The Cottagers

SHĀNA ŌSLER

Published by Editions BK
Rochester Hills, Michigan 48309
www.editionsbk.com

EDITIONS BK
BOOKS NEVER DIE

First Published 2023

Copy editor:
Barbara Battestilli, Oxford, Michigan

Printed and Manufactured in Poland by
Kozak Druk Siedlce

KOZAK DRUK

ISBN 978.0.578.27383.9

Library of Congress Control Number:
2023936499

Front Cover Image:
© Bruce Allen Kopytek 2023

Map of Mackinac Island:
© Bruce Allen Kopytek 2023

Back Cover Image:
© Frank Helsten, Helsingborg, Sweden 2023, Colorized by the artist.

To Stephen—
for reminding me
not to waste my time.

Acknowledgements

I'd like to thank all of the people who've encouraged me over the years, in particular my incomparable parents, Ken and Sharon Osler, and Grandma Jean, who liked to read my "stories." I want to thank Christina Karas, my critical reader, for her invaluable feedback and encouragement over the years, including with this book, and Carole Kopytek for thinking of its title! And especial thanks to my publisher, Bruce Kopytek, who took a chance on an unknown author and made this book possible. Thank you!!

One

People who knew Bertha Collins in Peoria thought her 'quite pretty;' her thick, raven curls had been much admired (not without grudge) at Rosewood Seminary, but never before today had anyone called her beautiful. Standing at the railing as the steamship chugged through the straits connecting Lakes Michigan and Huron, Bertha's youthful anticipation left an attractive impression. No feature warranted especial admiration. Her eyes were rather small and a forgettable shade of pale brown; her cheeks were a bit too round and her forehead too broad. Her thin lips had a nice color, which upon any woman with less pallid complexion would have been pleasant. She was of an average height and figure, which her traveling costume did little to enhance. And yet – the rosiest flush lit her round cheeks, her raspberry lips lifted in fetching smile and her pale skin seemed to glow as she gazed upon Mackinac Island. Those who saw her on the deck of the *S. S. Manitou* that afternoon regarded Bertha Collins as beautiful. Only her grandmother perceived this glowing, enraptured comeliness warily.

"That's her cottage – to the left of the big hotel," Bertha announced.

"Which one?" Mrs. Collins asked in resigned tone.

"Well, I'm not sure which one – but it's one of those big, white ones on that bluff left of the hotel . . . It might be the one on the far left – it's called Sunset Cottage, and that's the westernmost cottage. I'm sure the locals are familiar with it. They must be, for I intend to send Lillis my card in the morning. She'll want to know that we've arrived."

Mrs. Collins made no encouraging affirmation; she did not know whether Miss Lillis Halloran would be as enthused regarding their presence as Bertha intimated. She doubted that Miss Halloran's reception would live up to her granddaughter's expectation, but there was no tempering Bertha.

Poor Bertha was nine when Mrs. Collins had taken reluctant charge of her after her mother died in childbirth. Mrs. Collins had been strict in raising Bertha, but her methods had ceased to produce any effect after the girl left for boarding school. If not for her rheumatism and bilious constitution, Mrs. Collins might summon the strength to better manage her impetuous, strong-willed granddaughter, but she was simply too tired to make the required effort. Bertha insisted they spend the summer on Mackinac Island and here they were – two ladies from Peoria attempting to infiltrate the best of Midwestern society.

Mrs. Collins understood pride, but she knew its limitations. She had long been proud of her son – one of Peoria's most prominent citizens, and, for the last three years, an Illinois state senator. She had relished telling her friends of Bertha's exploits at the exclusive girls' academy. She had even – despite lamenting the excessive accounts of Miss Lillis Halloran over the last three years – been pleased to inform her friends that her granddaughter was a guest of the Joseph Hallorans when Bertha spent a weekend with them in Chicago last year. Yet her pride recoiled at their present circumstance.

Bertha had a legitimate acquaintance with Miss Lillis Halloran, but Mrs. Collins disapproved of her granddaughter's determination to foster the connection for social gain. It was vulgar and unlikely to yield the result she assumed Bertha hoped for. They were the first citizens of Peoria, but unknown to Chicago's fashionable set. And their destination – Mackinac Island – drew the cream of the Midwest's crop. Bertha was no great beauty, nor was she an accomplished musician, dancer or conversationalist. When Mrs. Collins looked upon her granddaughter's current radiance, she only thought of how much greater the contrast of defeat would seem; it made her tired and inflamed the rheumatism in her back.

Bertha took no notice of her grandmother's wary tone and frequent sighs. She couldn't believe she was really here! Gazing upon Mackinac Island – so close to Lillis' cottage! For years she had fed upon tales of cottage life; it seemed every girl at Rosewood Seminary had a cottage on Mackinac Island or Lake Geneva or some other exotic watering place. Of course Lillis Halloran should have the largest, most opulent cottage in the premier resort destination – and she would invite Bertha there for receptions and kettledrums and maybe even a dinner! They were, after all, intimately acquainted. Bertha had once been the Hallorans' houseguest for a weekend in Chicago and she had every reason to believe more invitations were forthcoming. She would garner introductions to Lillis' extended family and her island friends; by summer's end Bertha would be acquainted with the owner of every cottage along that west bluff – and maybe those on the east bluff, too! And she would charm them all, just like Lillis. She would be as lively and fun as Lillis and everyone on the island would adore her.

Elliott Maier's heart swelled in his chest as the steamer approached the central docks of Mackinac Island's small harbor. It seemed the feeling was reflexive and not tied to thought; he had experienced the same sensation upon first sight of the island as a boy and on every subsequent visit. And though it had been five long years since his last island stay, Elliott still smiled at first glimpse of Grand Hotel's porch preening from its majestic bluff top perch. He still felt that spark of excitement upon sight of the fort's long, graceful walls, though he knew the last soldiers had vacated the island the same summer he had. The soldiers had known they would never return; Elliott had still held out hope.

"Look, son," he pointed to the picturesque, white walls. "Fort Mackinac was built by the British. It's over one hundred years old."

"That's even older than Grandmother," Martin spoke with awed gravity. "It must have terrible neuralgia."

"Most definitely," Elliott agreed, managing to hide his laughter in a well-timed cough. "Fort Michilimackinac was originally built across the water there, but one year, the

Indians defeated the Brits in a great battle and captured the fort. The British won it back, but thought it would be safer to relocate to the island. And they stayed here, you know–even after the Revolution. It wasn't until after the War of 1812—"

"Are there still Indians here?" Martin cut to the most pressing concern.

"That was an interruption."

"Sorry," Martin's eyes fell – only for a second. "But are there?"

"Yes," Elliott returned. "But there will be no more battles – at least not here."

"So they're friendly?"

"Friendlier than they were one hundred years ago, at any rate."

"Can we visit the fort?" Martin asked hopefully.

"Yes."

"I'm going to find Daisy and tell her! I mean, may I—"

"Yes," Elliott nodded indulgently. "Go and find them. Try to lure them on deck to admire this view!"

Watching his towheaded eldest child skip up the deck, Elliott's heart seemed to constrict in the exact opposite reflex to that caused by the island views. He wanted his son to know and love the island like he had as a boy. Acknowledging the loss of this hope gripped Elliott with such profound sadness he imagined his very heart squeezed in pain. After all his losses in the past decade, Elliott found it nonsensical that forsaking the Mackinac Island cottage was the only occurrence able to physically affect his heart. But perhaps not, for his first great loss had also been here.

Adelia. Adelia Halloran – or Mrs. Alston, as she was now called. That was her cottage – that monstrosity of Gay Nineties opulence and ostentation queening over West Bluff Road. It had supplanted the smaller cottage owned by the Pond family back when Adelia still lived with her parents at Lakeview Cottage and his father built Mapleview Cottage across the boulevard. Back when their families met on the dusty road between cottages to walk to the Eating House for meals, he and Adelia always lingering behind the others. Back when he trusted no one more than Adelia with his confidences and thrilled to hear hers when she finally decided she could trust him. Back when the sight of her induced the same reflex that first sight of the island inspired and he wanted nothing more desperately in the world than to win a kiss from her sweet, rose lips. Adelia. Adelia Halloran . . . Alston?

"Martin says we're almost there?"

Elliott blinked, surprised to see his wife suddenly beside him, balancing little Walter on her hip as her powder blue eyes bore into his. Her eyes were merely honest and practical, but Elliott saw accusation in their depths. He heard reproof in her every word and saw blame in her expressions. He deserved her reproach; she had married a prosperous gentleman, the son of a state senator. They had both believed he would assume the mantle of bank president when his father retired and follow the old man into politics when duty called. But banks fail and politics is a fickle enterprise and wives have no one to blame but their husbands.

"Yes – can you feel the ship slow?" Elliott replied, as though her tone and look were perfectly benign. "We'll be docked in ten minutes."

"And there will be a carriage waiting? One that can accommodate us and our luggage?"

"If not, we'll hire a wagon for the luggage." He strove for a reassuring inflection of tone.

Iva seemed appeased; she turned away to drift up the railing toward Martin and Daisy. Elliott watched her go with equal measure of affection and aggravation. Iva was a good wife and mother, a fastidious housekeeper and exemplary hostess. She understood their financial difficulties and had immediately set to work economizing their household. She did not weep or succumb to hysterics or recklessly spend money as though nothing had changed. She was a right, little saint – a martyr. But just once, Elliott wished she would unleash her fury physically instead of tormenting him with that perpetually accusatory look. If only she would berate him instead of letting a tone of reproach overlay her every mundane phrase!

He hoped Iva's health improved with the island air. She contained her anger and indignation, so the emotions turned inward. They kept her up at night and induced nausea. Iva had lost so much weight since Walter's birth, she looked to Elliott as though a brisk breeze would send her floating over the ship's railing. Elliott had high hopes for that island air. The past six years had not been especially happy for the Maiers, but there had been some pleasant moments. Their road ahead might be bumpy, but they would traverse it. He must sell Mapleview Cottage, but his family would enjoy one last summer there.

Franklin Pruett sent his man ahead to ensure that the phaeton he had reserved for the summer awaited them, and to arrange transport for their luggage. Pacing the deck across the steamship's aft, Franklin looked over the island as though surveying a mine or inspecting a factory's floor. Mackinac was as picturesque as advertised. Grand Hotel had looked most impressive – from the water, at least. The sun shone and the crisp, fresh air acted upon his skin like a refreshing balm. She couldn't complain about the weather and she'd relish the cooler temperature. He wished she was here beside him to appraise this little island, but Franklin did not dare summon his wife before his man returned to confirm all was in order with their transport.

"Monty, Gil," he found his eldest sons leaning over the starboard railing, arguing about the clear water's depth at their present location. "Inform your mother that we are ready to disembark at her earliest convenience."

"I'll go," Gilbert offered, jogging off.

"Do you think it will work?" Montgomery's question caught his father off guard.

"Will what work?"

Meeting his son's dark eyes, Franklin felt unsettled by their shrewd expression. Montgomery was only fourteen, but he looked older today, and his powers of observation rivaled his father's. Here – on the starboard deck overlooking Mackinac Island – Franklin realized that his son would be a man one day, and that this was the first of many candid conversations he would be compelled to endure.

"Do you expect Mother to have such a jolly holiday here that she'll forget what you've done?" Montgomery's tone and glare were equally scornful.

"Of course I do not expect her to forget. This is about atonement."

"I wouldn't blame her if she divorced you," Montgomery declared, his cheeks flushing with sudden passion.

His son's rebuke stung Franklin, but he could offer no defense for his actions. He could not tell their son about Priscilla's refusal to share his bed. She didn't want to be "fat all my life" – that's what she told him when he had attempted to reclaim his marital rights just before Francis' first birthday; that was five years ago. Franklin couldn't confide to his son how Priscilla's indifference pained him, how he wanted her to know of his other women and give a damn about him again. But she knew – and worse than indifference was her understanding. She knew he was a passionate man and was perfectly content to let him seek his pleasure with other women – so she wouldn't be "fat." He yearned to explain all of this to his son, to redeem himself at least a fraction in his son's condemning eyes, but how could he explain to Monty that his mother's true grievance was not the transgression itself, but its discovery? His son must suffer through infatuation and young love, broken hearts and disillusion before he could hope to understand his parents' strained relationship.

To answer Monty's initial question – yes, Franklin thought it would work. Priscilla did not suffer broken heart or the shock of deception. Her pride, however, had endured a severe blow. And Franklin meant to rectify that. When Priscilla returned to Indianapolis she would dazzle her friends with tales of the fine people she had met this summer, her new wardrobe sent from Paris, and the Mackinac Island cottage her dear husband had acquired. Franklin was confident of his wife's forgiveness, but the realization brought him no comfort.

Mrs. Polly Easton surveyed the cows grazing on the sloping hillside opposite Grand Hotel's front lawn as the draft horses lumbered to pull their carriage up Cadotte Avenue. She opened her mouth to remark how little the landscape had changed since their last visit, but compressed her lips when she remembered that Verity wasn't speaking to her. Verity was often irate over some trivial slight, but she had not implemented the silent treatment in at least twenty years. The subject of their most recent quarrel hardly deserved the effort Verity exerted to prolonging it. As their carriage rolled to a stop beneath Grand Hotel's front portico, Polly determined to ignore her old friend's ill humor. Verity's fragile senses would not ruin *her* summer holiday.

Miss Verity Bennett watched her friend flounce up the porch steps through narrowed eyes. Polly's cruel insensitivity exacerbated her initial insult and Verity's ire grew with the realization that Polly had no intention of apologizing. The greatest moment of Verity's young life meant so little to Polly that she had likely already forgotten their quarrel's impetus.

It didn't help that Polly was tall and naturally slender and that Verity's doctor had recently advised her to lose weight if she wanted to surpass the age of sixty-five. Doctors were such dramatic creatures, and Verity still had four years before her sixty-fifth birthday – plenty of time to lose that weight. That was one of the reasons she had chosen Mackinac for their summer holiday; there wasn't much to do on the island that didn't involve at least mildly strenuous exercise. She intended to take up cycling and lawn tennis this year – she'd show that doctor who needed to lose weight! Though it would be nice – Verity paused to reflect at the top of the porch steps – to have the ability to climb more than six steps without heavy breathing; perhaps she needed to reevaluate her goals for the summer...

Verity's gaze swept the front porch with dismay. Spanning 660 feet, Grand Hotel claimed the distinction of possessing the world's longest front porch. When she and Polly first visited Grand Hotel six years ago in the summer of 1893, the porch had never been bereft of traffic. Ladies promenaded, showing off their latest fashions, and Army officers descended from the fort to parade their fine uniforms before those well-dressed ladies. A concert or demonstration drew guests to the porch's west end at least every other day. This grand aisle presiding over the Straits of Mackinac served as the social center of the island – the place to meet friends, to see and be seen. Yet now Verity had an unobstructed view to its east and west ends.

Only one other guest occupied the vast porch this afternoon – a stylish woman with artfully arranged ash-blonde tresses under an elaborately adorned hat. Her pained, matronly expression did not align with her delicately youthful features. She was either twenty-three or thirty-nine, with an aura of suffering as old as Eve. Verity determined to learn her history before the week's end.

By the time she approached the front desk, Polly had already signed the guestbook and had taken possession of the room keys.

"Room 206," Polly announced. "One of the western suites, as you requested."

Verity took her key with a slight nod; she may not be speaking to Polly, but her good breeding required the common courtesy of acknowledgment. She attempted to sweep away up the main staircase, but Polly's long legs soon overtook her. Verity gritted her teeth as she followed her friend up the west hall.

"Here we are," Polly proclaimed, unlocking the door and stepping into their suite. "I might have preferred one of the new east rooms—so much cooler and pleasant in the evenings—but I knew you wanted the sunset view. Each room seems equal in size and luxury; I'll take the yellow room and leave the lilac for you."

Polly waited expectantly, but Verity felt no compulsion to respond. Did Polly expect a medal for remembering that lilac was Verity's favorite color? This rare consideration hardly made amends for past affronts.

"I'll use the bathroom first, then," Polly declared. "I intend to bathe, but I'll be no more than an hour."

Verity drifted to the west-facing window as though she hadn't heard her friend.

"I'll be down for dinner at seven o'clock," Polly informed her.

Verity continued to gaze through the window, not deigning to acknowledge Polly's words. The cottages lining West Bluff Road impressed her. Some of them had been in various states of reconstruction on their last visit to Mackinac and several others she recognized as complete replacements of the original dwellings. Verity contemplated acquiring her own cottage on Mackinac Island. As she would no longer be traveling with Polly in summers, and she could not travel alone, Verity appreciated the value of a cottage with such inspiring views among such fine society.

Verity Bennett and Mary—or Polly, as everyone called her—Easton had been neighbors back in Bennettsville, Vermont. Of course Verity's home was the finer; the town was named for her paternal grandfather, a Revolutionary War hero. Polly's father was a lawyer and her grandfather owned the town's general store; she came from good yeoman stock, but lacked the Bennetts' refinement. Verity had always overlooked their difference in circumstance, for Polly had many admirable qualities. Polly's wit and beauty added the perfect adornment to Verity's noble poise. Even now—two dames in their sixtieth decade—Verity and Polly garnered admiration and respect.

Maintaining silence over dinner proved more difficult than anticipated. Verity was appalled by the vast, empty

Salle à Manger. Polly seemed perfectly content to gaze out the window. She put on a good show of nonchalance for their silent state, while Verity was nearly bursting to point out the ageless blonde from the porch.

This woman's gown was of exquisite taste. Her husband was a very handsome man – or was that her father? The two boys sitting on either side of her could be her brothers or her sons. In the dining room's soft light she looked nineteen or forty. She didn't seem to appreciate her companion's good looks – she never glanced his way. Verity turned to ask Polly what she thought, but promptly compressed her lips; she was not speaking to Polly.

"I'll share Allyne's room," Mrs. Webb spoke in tone of a soldier volunteering to lead the charge.

"Are you sure you're up to it, Patsy?" Mrs. Vandermeer drawled in tone denoting great skepticism.

Memories of the last week whirled through Allyne's mind as she watched her grandmothers spar before Grand Hotel's reception desk. Blood. Doctors. Hushed voices. Trains. Ships. And now here – Mackinac Island, the absolute middle of nowhere, edge of wilderness. Allyne was unimpressed with the Midwest's premier watering place and thought the only thing worse than her self-imposed social isolation would be for it to occur in a shared bedroom.

"I'll have my own room," Allyne announced. "The two of you can share or acquire another room. The hotel seems quite vacant."

Mrs. Vandermeer looked on edge of apoplectic fit, but Mrs. Webb's hand on her wrist checked the outburst.

"You know we can't leave you alone, Allyne," Mrs. Webb spoke in firm, yet soothing tone.

"I'll have my own room or step right back on the next ship to New York," Allyne declared, her pale cheeks flushing enough to give her grandmothers pause.

Patsy Webb met Allyne's dark eyes as she placed the room key into her granddaughter's gloved hand.

"Take the corner room at the far end of the third floor's west hall," Mrs. Webb spoke solemnly, as if sending Allyne off to attempt an arctic crossing. "We'll send Louisa up with your luggage."

Allyne felt the main staircase's slight slope and ascertained the time required to traverse half the length of the world's longest front porch. She found her room's furnishings too rustic for her taste and was dismayed to discover that she would have to leave her room and cross the public hall to use the bathroom. Tears filled Allyne's eyes as she realized that she could not stay here all summer.

But where could she go? No one spent summer in the city and she wouldn't dare be seen in Newport or any inch of Long Island. She would not subject herself to the snide smirks of her former friends or let her grandmothers' friends gaze upon her with pity. And she couldn't risk encountering Milton or Josie. Her grandmothers had hoped a year abroad would cure her heartache, but Europe had only exacerbated Allyne's pain and sense of betrayal. It seemed she had a fond memory involving Josie from every city they visited, unless it was a town she and Milton had planned to include on their wedding tour.

Allyne's eyes fell to the thin scab across her left wrist as she tugged off her gloves – a bleak reminder of why she was in the middle of nowhere at present. Stepping through the window, she grasped the railing of her small balcony and surveyed the splendid landscape. Afternoon sunlight dappled the sapphire water and molted the distant tree-lined shores. She drew in a deep breath of this "Eden-fresh" air and felt the island's calm essence envelop her. Allyne had read many accounts of Mackinac's pristine, remote beauty, beneficial health aspects, and timeless aura, but she had not appreciated any of those words until now. Perhaps she would stay here for the summer, after all.

Two

Miss Collins settled upon a rocking chair on the porch's west end – as far away from the rising sun as she could endeavor to be. As a child, Bertha ran wild over her grandparents' farm, her skin as brown as an Indian's. Lillis had a flawless, roses and cream complexion that Bertha had long tried to emulate with lemon juice rubs, wide-brimmed hats and parasols, and general aversion to outdoor activity. She had thus far demurred in all suggestions to explore the island, intent upon limiting her exposure to the dreaded, age-enhancing sun.

Lillis' response to Bertha's card had seemed promising. Bertha finally had the opportunity to visit Sunset Cottage as a guest at the Hallorans' reception last Wednesday. She had procured introductions to some of the island's best families, which she made good use of at the following night's hop in Grand Hotel's Casino. Yet five days had lapsed since then without further invitation from Lillis or the other cottagers.

Bertha had long been accustomed to sharing Lillis' time and devotion, and she appreciated how many varied acquaintances Miss Halloran possessed on Mackinac Island, but she had expected more of her friend's attention. Bertha had been naïve to think—with Lillis' broad acquaintanceship—that she would be sought out for every tea, drive or picnic. The disappointment of such high expectations might have discouraged more fragile souls, but only enhanced Bertha's determination to stand above Lillis' other friends.

Lifting today's edition of the *Resorter's Gazette*, Bertha diligently studied the pages. She would soon know all of the island families – their origins and occupations, if they possessed any eligible bachelors . . . Bertha's most earnest wish was to read her own name in the *Resorter's Gazette* connected to some glamorous reception or ball.

Mr. and Mrs. William Kearney and Miss Anne Kearney arrived at their cottage, Bella Vista, which overlooks Pontiac's Trail. Mr. Robert Kearney and Mrs. Kitty Kearney (née Halloran) remain on their European wedding tour, but are expected to visit Bella Vista before summer's end.

Bertha knew Anne Kearney; she hailed from Chicago and had been a year ahead at Rosewood. Bertha had never known greater satisfaction for an act of Providence – at least she was most satisfied with God for making Anne a year ahead of Lillis and her. When Anne left the seminary, Lillis had turned to Bertha to walk to classes with, to serve as audience for her guitar practice, to listen to her recitations as she memorized her lines. Yet the arrival of Miss Kearney on Mackinac Island did not perturb Bertha; Anne was another acquaintance she could leverage – another spoke in the wheel of Lillis' island society.

Mrs. Joseph Halloran hosted a reception for her daughter, Miss Lillis Halloran, at Sunset Cottage on Wednesday.

Bertha's heart skipped rapidly as she read Lillis' name in print – connected to an event she had attended!

Many of Miss Halloran's friends from their cottages or rooms at Grand Hotel attended the lively reception. From all accounts, the event lived up to Halloran standards.

Well, it had certainly been noisy and attended by so many people that the large home felt as though it might burst its seams.

Mr. and Mrs. Patrick Halloran opened neighboring Lakeview Cottage the day before their granddaughter's reception. Lakeview served as an auxiliary for Miss Halloran's guests.

Surely that was an exaggeration; the only "guests" Bertha had observed at Lakeview were the small assortment of husbands and fathers smoking on the cottage's veranda.

These Halloran cottages are located in a lovely community high upon the bluff west of Grand Hotel known as Hubbard's Annex. This neighborhood boasts some of the loveliest, most elegant cottages in the entire Middle West. Their proprietors enjoy cool lake breezes wafting over their gracious, tree-covered lots and spectacular vistas of the vivid Straits water. No doubt the island's calming, restorative effects are most prevalent from an Annex cottage veranda.

Bertha leaned back in her rocking chair, letting her eyes rest upon the indigo water. On this crisp morning, the water looked especially blue under the vast, cloudless sky. Her view marred by strolling strangers, Bertha agreed with the daily gazette – the vista would be far better from the veranda of one of those fine cottages along West Bluff Road or nestled in the cedar and pine-scented Annex.

Mr. and Mrs. Elliott Maier—with their young family—have reopened Mapleview Cottage for the first time in five years. The Maiers, of Kalamazoo, may have been kept away due to the closure of their bank and subsequent political defeats. Mapleview was built by Mr. Maier's late father, Michigan state senator Martin Maier, and was one of the original Annex cottages. Speculation is prevalent that Mr. Maier plans to sell Mapleview this summer.

Bertha read that last line again. An Annex cottage for sale! She would write to her father this very day and implore him to purchase it. Imagine her—Bertha Collins—a cottager! And her grandmother could give a reception for her in their new cottage, and invite Lillis and every other Annex resident!

Mrs. Elijah Alston, of Detroit, will host the season's first kettledrum at Pine Bluff this Wednesday. Mrs. Alston is the youngest daughter of Mr. and Mrs. Patrick Halloran, of Chicago. Her parents and brothers own some of the loveliest, most elegant cottages in the Annex, but Pine Bluff is by far the grandest. Situated on the bluff just west of Grand Hotel with a commanding view of the Straits, many consider Pine Bluff to be the island's most beautiful cottage. Mrs. Alston and her children opened the cottage in late June; Mr. Alston is expected to join them the last week of July.

Lillis had told Bertha quite a lot about her Aunt Adelia Alston. She was purported to be radiantly beautiful. Her husband came from a "lumber family," but had managed to triple his inheritance with shrewd investments and real estate transactions. All her gowns were sent from Paris. She scandalized her own family, and—according to Lillis—the Hallorans did not easily scandalize. Adelia bet money on cards, winning or losing hundreds of dollars in a single night. She smoked cigarettes and derived a mischievous joy from flavoring her punch and cordials with Halloran's Whiskey unbeknownst to her friends. Bertha had not been the only girl at Rosewood Seminary to hang on Lillis' every word when the subject was Adelia Alston. She must attend Mrs. Alston's kettledrum – she must! Bertha almost leapt from her chair, so overcome by her passionate resolve, but she exercised great discipline to finish the page – she couldn't miss anything important.

Miss Allyne Vandermeer of New York City arrived at Grand Hotel this week. Miss Vandermeer is accompanied by her grandmothers, Mrs. Vandermeer of New York and Mrs. Webb of Vermont. Miss Vandermeer's father, Mr. Randolph Vandermeer—one of the country's most prominent businessmen—may join his family in August if his business concerns afford him the time. Miss Vandermeer is recently returned from a year-long tour of Europe with her grandmothers. Mackinac Island is the farthest west Miss Vandermeer has ventured and no doubt the young ladies of the cottage community will keep her well entertained for the duration of her stay.

Bertha's gaze lifted from the page to observe the tall, willowy figure drifting past her rocker. From her exquisitely adorned hat to her perfectly tailored morning ensemble, by her flawless alabaster skin and heavy eyelids drooping with the weight of her fortune, Bertha recognized Miss Allyne Vandermeer. The solution to Bertha's social resolve literally walked right past her rocking chair. Bertha devoted the rest of her day to devising the means to procure an introduction to Miss Vandermeer.

Mr. Delbert Drury tipped the porter as handsomely as he dared; he felt as though he had traversed a mile from the reception desk – and he hadn't been carrying the bulk of his luggage. Del's gaze drifted dispassionately over the two twin beds to the slender wardrobes and through the narrow windows to the West Bluff cottages. This third floor, west-facing room would be stifling from three o'clock until at least several hours after sunset. Grand Hotel could hardly give its finest rooms to attendants of the Western Life Insurance agents' annual convention.

Del swiftly unpacked his luggage, glad to have first choice in both bed and wardrobe. He hoped his roommate wouldn't mind the encroachment into his wardrobe as they were far too small. The part of Del resigned to being an insurance agent scorned the part of him still clinging to hope. He may be in meetings much of the day, but he meant to cycle all over the island, try those new clay tennis courts on the front lawn, see about chartering a fishing boat and perhaps finagle a round of golf with one of the local club's members; he needed sporting costumes, his Norfolk suit and boater hat. There would likely be a hop or two in the evenings and Del was an excellent dancer; he needed at least two dinner jackets. Mackinac Island was the Midwest's version of Newport; it would be imprudent to leave his tails at home. All those elegant society ladies would be a delight to observe and might provide interesting scope –

"No," Del spoke aloud, interrupting the thought before it could materialize. "You're done with that."

Withdrawing the thin rejection letter from *Atlantic Monthly* from his breast pocket, Del viciously tore the paper in quarters and flung the remnants in the waste basket.

"From the wife or mistress?" a voice inquired through wheezing laugh.

Del hadn't noticed his roommate's arrival and the words startled him. He took a moment to conceal the repulsion that must have shone upon his face at the man's entrance. Fortunately the man seemed to attribute Del's expression to the discarded letter's contents.

"Merit Jones," he strode forward with extended hand that Del shook with the precise firmness and duration the occasion warranted; Del had always been conscientious about handshaking etiquette. "Muncie, Indiana."

"Del Drury, Indianapolis," Del flashed the man his best salesman smile – confident, yet unassuming, a smile inspiring trust and inviting confidences.

"First convention?" Mr. Jones assumed upon observation of his companion's smooth, young face.

"It is," Del nodded.

"My seventh," Mr. Jones proclaimed proudly. "I look forward to this week all year. It's the only week of peace for me in the year – so far away from Mrs. Jones and our little ones."

"How old are your children?" Del asked politely, all the while appalled that a man this fat—with cheeks that red and unkempt, russet beard that offensive—should have a wife, let alone offspring.

"Our oldest, Vi'let, is ten. Merit Jr. just turned eight. Zeke is four and our baby, Camellia—ain't that pretty? —she's eight months. Our other girl—Flora—died of pneumonia when she was just four, poor thing."

"I'm so sorry for your loss."

"She's with our Lord," Merit declared solemnly. "Have you already unpacked? Which wardrobe's mine, then?"

"Er – this one," Del opened the doors. "There wasn't room enough in the other for my garments. I hoped you wouldn't mind, but of course I can always remove—"

"Plenty of space left for my duds. But just how long did you plan on staying? The convention concludes Friday."

"I intended to stay through the weekend," Del declared.

"Just the one weekend?" Mr. Jones raised his bushy brows.

"I like to be prepared for any eventuality."

"I'll say," Mr. Jones whistled, hanging a dinner jacket next to Del's tails. "Very fine material, there."

"My late father's," Del acknowledged the fine coat.

"And I'm sorry for your loss. Was it recent?"

"Three years ago last March."

Mr. Jones finally seemed at a momentary loss for words.

"I'm going to inquire after a bicycle," Del announced. "I'll leave you to unpack."

"Is that what I have to look forward to?" Del muttered as he pedaled along the new gravel of the island's shore road. "A quadrupling of girth and proportional loss of hair? A life in which an insurance agents' convention is the highlight of my year?"

Yes, the realist overpowered the optimist to answer.

Del had once thought himself destined for finer things. He was one of Indiana's favored sons, but his father died suddenly near the end of Del's sophomore year at Princeton. His mother used a great deal of her inheritance to fund the last two years of Del's college, upon the understanding that

Del would support her after he graduated. The problem lay in Del's indecision; he could not decide what he wanted to be. Medicine would have been a stable, respectable career, but required too much schooling. The law—his father's profession—bored him. He had no head for business and lacked the ambition required to be an industrialist. Banking was worse than the law. The only thing Del had ever wanted to do was write – to moralize like Mark Twain, provoke like Dumas, inspire like James Fenimore Cooper.

But Del had finally relinquished these ambitions. The *Atlantic's* rejection was the last straw – the nail in his creative coffin. He could not continue to waste his time on prose when life demanded more of him. Or rather, he demanded more of life.

His mother had remarried last year; he was no longer responsible for her care or his younger sister's dowry, but the fact remained that he could not afford a morning coat, let alone new tails. He couldn't afford to buy a house or a nice phaeton – or new horse, for that matter. He had nothing to offer a lady, at least the type of lady he aspired to wed. As a writer there was a chance, but no worthy woman would accept a life insurance agent.

This bleak realization should have depressed Del, but as he pedaled along the island's west shore all defeatist thoughts and harsh realities evaporated in the sun's glow. Del watched the golden light's dancing reflection over the Straits. How could he despair in such a place – where every blade of grass invoked a smile and every cowbell, twittering bird and loon call was music to his ears? Del had read of Mackinac described as a "fairy island" and had already succumbed to its timeless magic. Yet he repressed these elated emotions, stomping over their potential. Never had a place so inspired him to write – just as he had determined to forsake writing!

"This is it," Del declared twenty minutes later, climbing Grand Hotel's porch steps.

Nothing else had panned out. When his Princeton friends retreated to New York, Del had followed – and exhausted his finances four months after graduation. No one wanted to publish Del's poems, essays or short stories. His mother no longer needed his support, but neither could she support Del. He must fend for himself as his father and grandfather had before him. His forebears had been far more successful in their endeavors; a life insurance agent was the best paying job Del had managed to procure. If that were not enough to thoroughly depress the soul, the nature of the business amply compensated. At least Del possessed a jovial enough nature to play the cards life dealt him, else he would have hung himself last summer.

Del's eyes met those regarding him as he stepped upon Grand Hotel's famous porch. They were the color of the sky on a June afternoon, set in a heart-shaped face like a lily. So struck by her beauty, it took Del a few seconds to perceive the fine cut and material of her evening gown. She was one of the elegant ladies he had hoped to observe this week, yet he had envisioned this study as subtle, even clandestine. He never imagined himself the object of reciprocal scrutiny. He couldn't address her. He couldn't even bow to her unless she acknowledged him first. She wanted to, but refrained. Hoping to see her in Grand Hotel's ballroom after dinner, Del strolled back to his room with considerably more buoyancy than he had demonstrated upon his exit.

Three

Flanked by her grandmothers, Miss Vandermeer drifted down the steps to the waiting carriages. Until now, she had been content to spend her time between meals in a porch rocking chair staring numbly over the water or seeking refuge in her room. Her heart ached as profoundly as the day Milton broke it; she still felt unworthy of love. But wallowing in despair did grow tedious and she was curious to see more of this lovely island. Earlier this morning, Grandmother Vandermeer came ready for battle and left the room flummoxed by Allyne's easy acquiescence to the proposed outing. Now they joined Grand Hotel's other guests who had signed on for the archeological tour.

A handsome man of middle age and three boys—most likely his sons—filled the first open landau. The boys' restless squirms made the carriage sway and dip. From the far corner of the rear-facing seat—her rigid posture more pronounced among her boisterous fellow passengers—an old woman with masses of gorgeous silver hair watched Allyne through vibrant, if discrete eyes. Her morning garb and hat were five years out of fashion, but did not detract from her austere, queenly air. Upon closer inspection, Allyne realized the woman did not regard her, but Grandmother Webb.

"The first two carriages are full," Mrs. Vandermeer observed in disapproving, indignant tone – how dare these Midwestern plebeians not offer the Vandermeers first choice of equipage!

Allyne noticed another older woman in the middle landau also studying Grandmother Webb with intensity uncommon to sight of persons unknown.

"Are you acquainted—"

"There's room in the third carriage," Mrs. Webb spoke over her granddaughter. "Lydia, why don't you and Allyne join those in the third vis-à-vis and I'll fill the middle landau's empty place."

Before Mrs. Vandermeer or Allyne could protest, Mrs. Webb had taken the groom's hand and stepped up into the middle carriage.

Turning to the last open landau, Allyne's gaze fell upon the girl occupying the far corner of the rear-facing bench. Her features were inoffensive, though her morning jacket's puffed sleeves had gone out of fashion three years prior. She sat across from—rather than beside—her elderly companion. Allyne guessed the girl to be at least three years her junior – certainly old enough to know how rude it was to stare. Allyne was accustomed to admiring glances, but felt disconcerted under this young woman's vividly feasting eyes. Her gaze flitted elsewhere as any other's would, but the intensity of the looks in between gave Allyne the odd sensation of drowning. She didn't want to sit next to this strange girl, but Grandmother Vandermeer had already settled upon the forward-facing bench. Allyne reluctantly grasped the groom's hand to propel her into the third landau's only vacant seat. She fixed her eyes on the strip of horizon visible between the peninsula tips, her posture as aloof and proper as Grandmother Vandermeer in her loftiest mood.

"Good morning!" his robust greeting drew Allyne's attention to the slight, little man hovering on the porch steps. "Jimmy Hayes welcomes you for today's archeological tour! For those of you I've not yet had the privilege of meeting, I am this grand hotel's proud manager.

"Mackinac Island is a fascinating archeological specimen. Your knowledgeable guides will tell you what is known of its formations, their origins and legends. You'll return in time for afternoon tea, though I expect you may feel too full to partake after your excellent picnic lunch! I look forward to hearing your opinions of these curious limestone formations in the coming days. But I have delayed you long enough! I bid you adieu, bon voyage – happy exploring!"

His confident, promising tone made Allyne forget his balding pate and how his mustache unbecomingly dominated his thin, lively face. Yet she distinctly perceived Mr. Hayes's droop of shoulder and sigh of relief as their carriage wheels ground to life over the drive. He had only been acting – putting on a brave show; Allyne recognized her fellow artist.

Her gaze fixed upon the brilliantly blue water, Allyne didn't register many of their driver's words other than to observe how uncanny it was to suddenly realize that the driver was in close enough proximity for speech, and that he presumed his passengers cared to hear his speech.

"Good day." Allyne watched her grandmother shudder with disapproval as the dowdy old woman beside her impinged upon her social better without invitation. "It is a very fine day for this tour – isn't it? I'm Mrs. Collins, and may I present my granddaughter, Miss Bertha Collins?"

Mrs. Vandermeer politely—in discouraging, yet refined tone—returned the greeting and introduction. Mrs. Collins perceived the nature of this response and both women turned their full attention to the driver's description of a rock formation called Sugar Loaf. Miss Bertha Collins, however, had only been waiting for this introduction to pounce upon her prey.

"Is this your first summer on Mackinac?" Bertha inquired.

"Yes," Allyne replied, glad that sitting beside the girl meant she could avoid her eyes without appearing rude.

"It's my first summer here, too," Miss Collins acknowledged. "Though I've heard so much about the island from Lillis, I feel I know it as well as any cottager."

She waited expectantly for Allyne to ask who Lillis was; Miss Collins swallowed her disappointment and answered anyway.

"My dear friend, Lillis Halloran. Her family has a cottage in the Annex. Actually, they have three Annex cottages – between her father, uncle and grandparents. Her Aunt Adelia's cottage on West Bluff Road is said to be the prettiest on the island. But I'm sure you're acquainted with the Hallorans."

"Why should you be sure of that?" Allyne frowned.

"Your dress is as fine as any of Lillis'," Miss Collins

dropped a well-planted compliment. "I'm sure it's from Paris, but assumed you knew the family from Chicago?"

"I've never been to Chicago."

"Good heavens – I feel silly! Forgive me, Miss Vandermeer. Where are you from?"

"New York."

"What a fine city! I've never been, but Lillis has told me of its vastness and vibrancy. She also confided that most of her clothing—that not from Paris—she purchased in New York."

"Your friend sounds very well dressed," Allyne offered through twitching lips.

"Oh, she is," Miss Collins failed to notice her companion's ridicule. "Mackinac Island is so far from New York."

"Though not . . ." Allyne smiled, for the first time in over a year, ". . . so far as Paris."

"Have you any acquaintances on the island?"

Miss Collins' question erased Allyne's smile, but only for a moment. Who was Bertha Collins, after all, for Allyne to feel embarrassed before? For that matter – who was Queen Lillis? Allyne would never see these Midwesterners after this summer. She had never before conversed with a contemporary whose favorable opinion didn't matter.

"None," Allyne declared. "My grandmothers and I have no western connections."

"You poor dear!"

Bertha's exclamation made Allyne's grin broaden; no one had ever called her poor before.

"I'd be happy to arrange an introduction to Lillis. She's acquainted with nearly everyone on the island. She'll no doubt see that you're invited to every reception and social event – at least the best ones."

"I'd only want to attend the best ones," Allyne declared in well struck imitation of Grandmother Vandermeer.

"Naturally," Miss Collins nodded, her tone equally pompous.

"Halloran..." Allyne's brow furrowed in thought. "I know I've never met a Halloran, but why do I know the name?"

"Halloran Fine Tobacco and Spirits," Miss Collins announced without a trace of shame for her exalted friend. "Her grandfather founded the company."

Allyne's gloved fingers rose to her lips to suppress a giggle. Mackinac Island's first family had their money from liquor and tobacco! Miss Lillis' grandparents probably grew up rooting for potatoes in Ireland just like all of their maids and grooms back in New York. And yet Allyne still wished to meet her. Thought of being dependent upon Miss Bertha Collins for her summer society gave rise to another chuckle, which she turned into a remark upon Arch Rock's beauty.

Mrs. Polly Easton's curious gaze traveled from the view to her driving companions as their landau rolled languidly away from Arch Rock. She saw the majestic limestone arch until the overhanging tree limbs concealed the view – for Polly sat upon the rear-facing bench; she wouldn't risk a glimpse of Verity's scowling façade in the first carriage marring these splendid views. With the arch lost to the trees, Polly turned her attention back to Madonna and Child on the opposite bench.

The child was nine or ten, so Polly knew Mother must be near thirty (though she looked so young! With that smooth, porcelain skin and wide eyes the color of the Michigan sky). They looked like sisters, with fine, delicate features and the same heart-shaped face. Daughter had thick, silky mahogany hair; Mother's thick, silky tresses were a pale ash-blonde. Both seemed very attentive to the gentlemen sharing Verity's carriage.

While Polly studied Madonna and Child—trying to recall their names and where they had claimed to hail from—she had the uneasy sensation of being watched. Polly perceived how often the woman sitting beside her turned to regard her profile – and stole almost as many return glances. Inevitably, they turned at the same time and their eyes widened in simultaneous recognition.

"Patsy Miller!" Polly cried.

"Polly Crawford! Of all the – can it really be you?"

"It's me, though I'm Polly Easton now."

"Of course – I heard… I'm so sorry for your loss."

"Thank you," Polly nodded as solemnly as if the sentiment had been uttered months rather than decades after her husband lost his life in service of the Union Army. "And I should have remembered that you're Mrs. Webb now. Everyone in town remembers your wedding."

"Are you still in Bennettsville?"

"I moved to Michigan to be closer to my son ten years ago," Polly informed her old acquaintance. "But just last summer I returned to Bennettsville to visit Verity."

"Verity Bennett?" Patsy looked as if she remembered Verity well, though not necessarily fondly. "Did she ever marry?"

"No; no one was ever good enough for a Bennett, but if you ask her about it, she'll likely blame me for her spinsterhood."

"She's not—?"

"Oh, yes – the grand dame herself presides over the first carriage."

"But why—" Patsy checked herself before completing the question, but Polly had long ago shed East Coast reserve for Midwest candor.

"We traveled here together; we're sharing a suite, but Verity isn't speaking to me at present."

"Why the uncharacteristic reticence?" Patsy ventured.

"For no good reason, though it's of great significance to Verity."

"You always were the best of friends – like sisters. Her present mood aside, it's nice that you're traveling together after so many years."

"We've summered together every year since I left Vermont."

"Do you always visit Mackinac Island? Or do you rotate between Michigan and Vermont?"

"Oh, no – last year was my first venture back to Vermont since moving here, and we've only been to the island once before. Two years ago we explored the Canadian Maritimes, we lazed away the previous summer at Saratoga Springs, and the year before that we took a proper European tour. We've been to Newport, the Cape, Niagara Falls and Toronto, and one summer we toured the English and Scottish countryside."

"And of all those destinations, Mackinac Island is the only one you've returned to?" Patsy asked, her tone somewhat incredulous.

"Verity deemed the air quality here to be superior to any place she's visited, and I'll not argue when her chosen resort is a mere day's sail from home. We enjoyed our first stay here very much – that was the summer of '93. It did seem a great deal livelier that summer, but perhaps it's still early in the season. But enough about us! What brings you so far west? And who is that lovely young lady I saw you walking with?"

"My granddaughter, Allyne. My son-in-law's mother, Mrs. Lydia Vandermeer, and I are accompanying her this summer."

"And your daughter? Is she busy with Allyne's younger siblings?"

"Alice – we lost Alice the day after Allyne was born."

"I'm so sorry!" Polly flushed with shame. "How indelicate of me! I'm always blurting things out without thinking. Do forgive me?"

"There's nothing to forgive – you could not have known."

Though Polly *had* known. Bennettsville was a small town. Patsy may have left Vermont forty years ago, but her brothers and sister still lived there. Everyone in town had heard of Alice Webb's triumphant society marriage and death from childbirth only a year later.

"Are you enjoying the island so far?" Polly swallowed her shame to ask.

"I am. It's so peaceful and remote – and I agree with Verity about the air quality. I'm afraid it's a bit rustic for Lydia, but so long as Allyne enjoys it, we'll stay."

Polly turned to observe the fort's white buildings to conceal her reflexive frown. Whoever heard of a young girl's preferences superseding her grandparents'? No doubt Patsy spoiled her – Allyne was all she had left of her only daughter. But overindulging children never did them any good. Polly was only blessed with one child before her dear John was killed in the war, but she had used a firm hand raising their son. Polly was proud of her strict, but fair parenting tactics, for she had reared a strong, self-reliant and honorable man. John would be proud if he could see his namesake now – a self-made lumber baron with a charming wife and three beautiful, well-behaved children. But Polly had no wish to speak of these sentiments to Patsy; she was too grateful for the conversation after so many days of silence to risk offending her.

"Why are you angry with Father?" Madonna's child murmured under their driver's tale of Robinson's Folly.

"Emmeline," the woman—Mrs. Pruett, that was her name—reprimanded her daughter in hushed, yet fierce tone. "You do not speak of personal matters in public. How many times must I tell you this? And—" her sky blue eyes flitted up briefly to Polly's. "—I am not angry with your father."

"But you haven't—"

"Emmeline!" Mrs. Pruett implored.

"Emmeline – what a pretty name," Patsy intervened to save Mrs. Pruett further embarrassment. "Where have you and your mother traveled from?"

"Indianapolis," the girl replied in shy voice, suddenly aware of the two strangers.

"You must have many friends in Indianapolis, but have any of them ever been fortunate enough to summer on an island?"

"Florence Anderson visited Mackinac Island last summer, but she was only here for two weeks. That was all her family could afford."

"Emmeline!" Mrs. Pruett groaned.

"How old are you, Emmeline?" Polly asked.

"Eight – I'll be nine in December. How old are you?"

"Good gracious, Emmeline," Mrs. Pruett hissed.

"A legitimate question," Polly excused the girl's impetuous question – always sympathetic to a fellow blurter of truths and awkward inquiries. "I turned sixty-one in June and do you know that I haven't seen Mrs. Webb in forty years! But when we were eight like you we saw each other every weekday in school and every Sunday at church."

"Thank you," Mrs. Pruett favored Polly and Patsy with an angelic smile. "You're both so gracious. I couldn't help overhearing your remarkable exchange earlier. How wonderful to meet an old friend from childhood in such a faraway place."

They chatted amicably as the landaus rolled around Mission Point, though Mrs. Pruett lost her train of thought mid-sentence when the cyclist pedaled past their carriages. Polly decided to forgive Mrs. Pruett's distraction. The socks below his knickerbockers revealed sculpted, muscular calves and his broad shoulders filled out his sporty Norfolk jacket quite well. His straw boater perched over a fine head of chestnut hair. Polly never glimpsed his face, but by profile and rear view thought him quite a fine male specimen. Mrs. Pruett was too old to let his appearance so distract her – certainly too old for that girlish blush staining her cheeks, but she did have Polly's sympathy.

After returning his rented bicycle to the shop, Del Drury strolled up the broad avenue toward the hotel – uncharacteristically unaware of his surrounding landscape. The sky made him think of her eyes, and their appraising, admiring gleam. She was the type of lady who most intrigued him – the kind whose aloof elegance and cultivated beauty he found alluring, whose sophistication seduced his fervent mind and whose ability to create their own perception fascinated him.

Del had recognized the girl beside her in the carriage as her daughter and he suspected the debonair gentleman in the first carriage as the likely culprit of husband. The three boys with him were probably her sons and the refined, silver-haired woman, her mother. She was a married, middle-aged mother of four and Del wanted her more than he had ever desired a woman. A dozen narratives with her as heroine flitted through his mind as Del drifted up the raised boardwalk to the hotel.

"Excuse me?" Del approached the front desk clerk. "Has the archeological tour returned?"

"No, sir. They're due back at three-thirty."

Del should be in the Casino listening to the success stories of Western's top grossing agents. He should be seeking tips and advice from his fellow insurance agents, making new acquaintances, committing himself to his chosen career. Instead he claimed a rocker just west of the porch steps and peered over the top of his newspaper, watching for the three landaus he had sped past at Mission Point.

His head snapped up hopefully each time he heard the jangling tack of an approaching pair. He regarded his watch after each carriage rumbled past – the tour was now fifteen minutes late in their return. Detecting the booming voice and wheezing chuckle of his roommate conversing with an equally pathetic companion, Del lifted the newspaper to hide his face. He kept it raised until Merit Jones' voice was far enough to be indistinguishable. Upon lowering the paper, he saw the occupants of the tour's first carriage mounting the steps.

Del kept the paper raised and tried to affect a relaxed posture as he discretely observed them. Those were undoubtedly her sons. The oldest—a strapping sixteen-year-old—possessed a masculine echo of his mother's features with his father's dark eyes. His younger brothers looked like their father, who—Del grudgingly acknowledged—was a handsome man. Though his bearing was arrogant to an unbecoming point of pomposity – and why hadn't he waited beside the second carriage to offer his arm to his wife? Instead he strode carelessly beside his sons, leaving his little daughter to escort his wife. He was clearly unworthy of such a lady.

Del dropped all pretense of subtlety to watch her ascend the steps. Her flawless face rose above her slender neck like a lily. To kiss such a delicate nose and pointed chin, such plush rose lips and smooth, narrow forehead . . .

Del's heartbeat accelerated when her wide-set, blue eyes met his over the top of his newspaper. He thrilled to see the flush rise to her cheeks as her lashes swept down to hide her eyes and a sudden lurch gripped his stomach – for he recognized her! He had seen this woman and her husband at his step-father's house during some holiday entertainment.

Del let his arms drop, the paper crinkling over his legs as he wavered between complete dejection and utter hysteria. She must have recognized him from the same function – that was why she met his eyes so often. She likely thought she recognized him, but—as he was such an insignificant object in her orbit—couldn't recall his name.

Del made to rise from the rocking chair, but stayed his movement to observe the third carriage's passengers. He knew that young lady – the tall, willowy figure with impossibly long neck and desultory eyes. A sophisticated society lady in her infancy: Allyne Vandermeer – what literary potential she already exuded at such a young age! Del had encountered her at many a New York entertainment. Her cousin, William, had been Del's best friend at Princeton; Miss Vandermeer was present at every New York reception or dance William had secured an invitation for him to attend. Del waited for Allyne Vandermeer to acknowledge him as she climbed the porch steps, but she drifted past him through the front doors without a glance.

Four

Elliott Maier paused halfway through his shearing of the hopelessly overgrown front yard to admire the painters' progress. Mapleview Cottage had been in more dire state than anticipated. The roof needed re-shingling, woodland had reclaimed most of the yard and the cottage's interior showed its age, but all Elliott could afford to address were the exterior walls. At this moment—with the afternoon sun slanted over the surrounding cedars—its walls were the exact shade of robin's egg blue he remembered from his halcyon adolescence. Half a lifetime ago this cottage had been new and shining and proud. Back when nothing had seemed so real as cedar-scented air, crisp blue skies and glimpses of Adelia Halloran waltzing along the gracious veranda across the street.

Technically, Lakeview Cottage was kitty-corner to Mapleview. The original Halloran cottage—a simple Caskey design gradually inflated over the last decade—perched upon the southwest bluff top at the curve of Lakeview Boulevard. Mapleview's official address was on Park Street.

In his mother's reign, Mapleview's meticulously trimmed yard had been enclosed in hydrangea hedges. Potted ferns had crowded the porch and scarlet geraniums lined the front steps. Elliott's eyes lifted to the front gable window, half expecting to see his sister Laura's face emerge from the fluttering lace curtains. Poor Laura had wept when he told her he must sell their cottage.

Girlish laughter drifted over from Lakeview Cottage's veranda. Elliott's head snapped up at the sound; he knew it wasn't her, but she haunted him. That heady laugh—so superior to her companion's giggle—was an echo of Adelia's teen voice. Peering over the overgrown hydrangeas, Elliott recognized Lillis Halloran and her cousin, Alva. Those girls were still in pigtails the last time he saw them.

"Elliott Maier?"

Elliott finally noticed the man standing at his front gate and hastened forward for a hearty handshake.

"Hugh Pendleton! It does me good to see you again!" Elliott grinned at his favorite island chum.

"Never thought I'd see you again. Then Agnes read in the *Resorter* that you had returned."

"Did they mention the bank failure and that I'm the son of a former state senator?"

"Yes, I believe they did."

Elliott's good-natured grin removed any embarrassment or shame from the situation and put his old friend at ease.

"They also say you've only come back to sell the place," Hugh's tone sobered. "I hope that's not true?"

"I'm afraid it is," Elliott acknowledged. "And I own I'm impressed with the *Resorter's* reporters. They could only have gleaned that information from the park's superintendent, but then I did ask him to connect me with potential buyers, so I can't be cross, can I? I've had to eat a lot of crow in the last six years, Hugh. I've very little pride left. It's actually quite liberating. But enough with reality – I'm devoting the next two months to forgetting it. One last glorious summer on the island!"

"Will you give Mrs. Maier Agnes's card?"

"Of course," Elliott tucked the offered card into his pocket.

"She'd like to give a reception for Mrs. Maier."

"Iva would be honored, and after I present this card, she'll hasten to call upon Mrs. Pendleton to express her gratitude."

"Hang it – I heard you studied the law, but do you talk like a lawyer now?" Hugh chided.

"Bad habit," Elliott laughed. "And Iva's influence. She's—ah—very conscientious, especially of social matters. But even before our wives observe the proprieties, our children should meet."

"I think I have one for every age of yours – plus the older boy to watch over them all. Should I send them over this afternoon?"

"Best let me prepare mine first – and they have too many chores yet to finish today. Tomorrow after breakfast?"

"Done."

"And Hugh – let's take the boys fishing? Let's sail out to the Les Cheneaux Islands and sleep under the stars like we used to with our fathers."

"We'll have the full experience – when Father hears about our plan, he'll insist on coming."

"I'd love to see him."

"We'll schedule around the women's reception plans, of course."

"Of course," Elliott's smile stretched as he bid his old friend good day.

Bolstered by the encounter, Elliott found renewed strength in his aching, underutilized muscles. He finished cutting the grass and pulled up three saplings before setting to work pruning the hydrangea hedge.

Elliott clipped the rounded corner hedge when he became aware of the figures strolling up Lakeview Boulevard. Letting his arms fall slack, he straightened his sore, strained back and squinted in the late afternoon sun to observe the approaching women. By the time he recognized Mrs. Halloran, it was too late to discretely retreat. Elliott felt obliged to stand his ground as Adelia's mother and her companion approached.

Mrs. Halloran looked the same as he remembered her, aside from her scornful expression. The Hallorans aged well – at least their exteriors aged well. Elliott knew Mrs. Halloran was ten years older than his mother, but she looked ten years younger. He had always thought hers a warm, jolly disposition, so the hard look in her wide, brown eyes and lips thinned in straight line of disapproval unsettled him. Of course she must despise him now; she had good reason.

"Elliott Maier," Mrs. Halloran paused to meet his eyes over the hydrangeas.

"Mrs. Halloran," Elliott bowed. "How pleasant to see you."

"I hear you're selling Mapleview?" Mrs. Halloran raised her thin, black brows.

"Yes."

"I'm glad to hear it," she paused just long enough for Elliott to perceive her true sentiment. "This lot has been an eyesore these last few years. I'll be glad to see this cottage lived in once more. Our cottages should be loved, don't you think?"

"Yes," he nodded.

"And if one family can no longer maintain it, the cottage deserves a family better equipped to its care."

Her words lashed Elliott like a flogging whip, but he was saved from responding by Iva's appearance. His wife pushed through the screen door, balancing Walter upon her hip as she descended the porch steps. Elliott admired his wife's poise as she faced the older women with proud tilt to her chin. Iva's evanescent beauty still clung to her pale blue eyes and smooth façade. Her limbs were so slender and her hair so ghostly gray-blonde, she possessed an aspect of frailty that was absent from her unflinching gaze just now.

"Mrs. Halloran, may I present Mrs. Maier?" Elliott offered the required introduction.

"Mrs. Maier," Mrs. Halloran nodded curtly to Iva's slight bow. "I hope you're enjoying our island?"

Mrs. Halloran's tone was unconsciously proprietary. Mackinac was the Hallorans' island. The Indians had the more legitimate claim and the French fur traders and British fishermen had called the island theirs long before the Hallorans decided to build cottages and invest in a golf club there, yet it was still the Hallorans' island. (At least according to the *Resorter's Gazette* and current real estate holdings.)

"My daughter, Adelia Alston, is entertaining next Thursday," Mrs. Halloran informed Iva. "I'll be sure you receive an invitation. Good day."

"Good day," Iva murmured, watching the older women drift up the avenue before turning reproachful eyes upon her husband.

"Should I be flattered?" Iva asked once Mrs. Halloran and her un-introduced companion were safely out of earshot. "She made the invitation sound like a royal bequest."

"The Hallorans are rather like island royalty," Elliott acknowledged.

"Is she an old friend of your mother's?"

"No."

"Why not?" Iva pried, keeping her eye on Walter as he ran heedlessly over the freshly cut grass. "They were neighbors, and I presume your mother would have been quite interested in fostering a royal friendship?"

"The Hallorans are Catholic," Elliott explained.

"Surely a political family is friends to all faiths?" Iva quipped.

"Mother was livid every time they had a Sunday entertainment – and that was about once a week. Old Mr. Halloran has a yacht moored at the base of that bluff across the street. The extended family sail it to St. Anne's and back for Mass every Sunday and carry on with a dinner or lawn games or even a dance when they're feeling restless."

"Heavens; I hope they're not loud," Iva frowned.

"Oh, you'll hear them. But what Mother most objected to were the Halloran Fine Tobacco and Spirits prevalent at these Sunday entertainments."

"Ah – that's where I've heard the name. Didn't your father run on a temperance ticket?"

"Precisely."

"Ought I to accept this invitation to Mrs. Halloran's daughter's entertainment?" Iva asked in rare deferment of a social matter.

"You should," he nodded, hoping she hadn't noticed his slight hesitation. "All the best ladies on the island will be there. Speaking of..." Elliott withdrew Agnes Pendleton's calling card from his pocket and handed it to Iva.

"Hugh's wife – he was my closest friend on the island. Their cottage, Pendleton Pines, is on Holt Avenue, just behind us. Their oldest boy, Thomas, is nine; then he has one for each of ours. William is seven like Martin, Lily is five like Daisy, and their youngest—Angelica—is six months older than Walter. Hugh says Agnes would like to host a reception for you."

"I'll call on her tomorrow," Iva nodded.

Iva was ever acquiescent; she always did the right and proper thing and acted in a manner most beneficial to the Maiers. No dangerous, fiery streak in her; no delightfully impetuous or silly antics from her. Elliott realized how fortunate he was in his wife, but he'd like her so much more if she let herself enjoy the day instead of sacrificing herself to its hours.

“I don’t think Grandmother Vandermeer is much impressed with Grandmother Webb’s old friends,” Allyne remarked to her maid Friday afternoon. “A little tighter, Lou.”

Louise Cooper gave the corset laces a half-hearted tug before tying them. “If I lace you any tighter there will be gaps in the waist.”

“Did Grandmother Webb tell you to say that?” Allyne demanded, her face flushing with emotion.

“No one needs to say anything,” Lou’s Brooklyn drawl predominated over her practiced pronunciation. “I care for your dresses and can’t help but notice you’ve lost a considerable amount of volume since these frocks were commissioned.”

“Do you mean to complain of the extra labor involved in the minor alterations a few of my garments may require?” Allyne’s narrowed eyes met her maid’s in the mirror.

“Oh, no, Miss Allyne,” Lou’s reverent tone and faux somber expression drew Allyne’s grudging chuckle. “So what does Mrs. Vandermeer have against Mrs. Webb’s friends?”

“Grandmother Webb is from Bennettsville, Vermont. She knew Mrs. Easton and Miss Bennett from their school days in that small town.”

“And Mrs. Vandermeer’s objections?” Lou prompted.

“They are strange, you know,” Allyne confided. “They’re traveling together, but aren’t on speaking terms. Mrs. Easton says Miss Bennett hasn’t said a word to her in seventeen days. And they won’t tell anyone what prompted their quarrel. Do you know, I rather admire them – to inspire such intrigue at sixty years old... Though their behavior was quite ridiculous. Our dinner last night was most awkward and their refusal to converse irritated Grandmother Vandermeer's nerves.

"I'm determined to learn why Miss Bennett won't speak to Mrs. Easton. I know Miss Bennett considers the cause of great significance, while Mrs. Easton believes it inconsequential. Do you know they've been friends for over fifty years? I don't have a single friend I'd care to see in ten years, let alone fifty. Do you?"

"Can't say that I do," Lou responded promptly as she secured the last button of her mistress's stylish afternoon dress. "Though I gather you've found a new friend to inspire such care for your afternoon attire?"

"Bertha Collins is hosting an afternoon tea," Allyne explained.

"Miss Collins – from Peoria?" Lou's worldly, gray eyes reflected her mistress's natural scorn for such places as Illinois.

"She's promised an introduction to Miss Lillis Halloran, the island's princess. Most of these cottagers are from Chicago and western Michigan."

"It might be nice," Lou remarked casually as she pushed a pearl-tipped hatpin through her mistress's chapeau. "To meet a new crowd – where every face is new and each relationship a blank slate to be written on this summer."

"Yes," Allyne acknowledged thoughtfully. "I rather like that sentiment. And I suppose I should leave now so the first words on this slate do not involve how inconsiderately late I was to our inaugural tea."

Allyne's initial reaction to Bertha's lavish setting required swiftly raised gloved fingers to suppress outward display of laughter. Miss Collins had reserved the rounded western end of the great porch. Ropes enclosed the spacious section and a guard in hotel livery manned the entrance. Did Miss Collins genuinely fear the riffraff, otherwise known as "Transients" – those unfortunate souls who could only afford a week's rate at Grand Hotel? Or were the ropes there to bring greater attention to the exclusive ensemble within? Allyne strongly suspected the latter.

As Allyne swept majestically past the guard to join the three ladies gathered around the tea table, a crisp northwest breeze caressed her cheeks and blew away her inhibitions. The fresh air—heady with scent of lake and pine—aroused her sense of adventure. She didn't mind what that lurking reporter wrote about her in the local papers; no one important would read it. Allyne had no care for what these ladies thought of her, and yet the prospect of impressing them appealed to her. These ladies didn't know her mother had been a humble solicitor's daughter who died before she could tell Allyne anything useful. They didn't whisper about how much more devoted her father was to Wall Street than his own daughter. They didn't know Josie Van Buhler or Milton Jones or the story of how they broke Allyne's heart.

"Miss Vandermeer," the swell of Bertha's pride lifted her from her chair at Allyne's approach. "May I present Miss Halloran and Miss Kearney, both of Chicago?"

"Here we're just Lillis and Anne of Mackinac Island," Lillis' smile disarmed Allyne.

So this was the infamous Lillis Halloran – and she exceeded every expectation. Her blonde beauty was exquisite, yet friendly. Allyne couldn't resent those jade green eyes or flawless, porcelain skin, but if she could have chosen her own features they would closely resemble Miss Halloran's. And charm! The lady exuded such subtle, yet powerful charisma. She was humble and self-deprecating while flaunting Parisian dress and the most gorgeous hat Allyne had ever beheld. She was friendly, but with a degree of aloofness that made Allyne feel privileged to count her as an acquaintance. Lillis drew laughter with wit rather than vulgarity and spoke only enough to leave her audience in want of more. Allyne—accustomed to snide comments, veiled insults or general disregard from eastern society—could not help feeling flattered that a lady like Lillis Halloran exhibited such interest in forming a friendship. Miss Halloran's demeanor indicated a lack of care or knowledge of Allyne's fortune and her father's prominence, leaving Allyne to conclude Lillis' interest was motivated by herself and not her circumstances.

"I want to learn tennis this summer," Lillis announced, spreading lemon curd over a scone. "Does the Grand offer lessons – do you know?"

"I'll inquire," Miss Collins was quick to offer.

"Do you play, Miss Vandermeer?" Lillis asked.

"No, I've never had an inclination. And do call me 'Allyne'."

"Do you cycle, Allyne?"

"No," Allyne shook her head. "I ride, of course. And I golf a little."

"A golfer!" Lillis cried, her beauty condensing with her bright smile. "You must play with me! I've no companions with Kitty gone."

"Is there a course on the island?" Allyne inquired. "And Kitty?"

"My sister, Kitty – she married Anne's brother, Rob, last month. She was my only fellow golfer here, but she's on her wedding tour. It's not much of a course, but we have a few links for Annex cottagers. I don't have a card with me, but if you write to me at Sunset Cottage with your availability, I'll reserve time for us on the course.

"I do have," Lillis withdrew two cards from her reticule, "invitations to Aunt Adelia's kettledrum this Thursday."

Allyne was struck by the reverence with which Miss Collins accepted the invitation; Bertha's cheeks glowed with sense of success and finally Allyne felt at ease with the present dynamic. They had all been so cordial, so kind, so deferential – Allyne's social training had taught her to look for cause of behavior, and no one in Allyne's experience ever acted without endeavor to affect a response or circumstance. Lillis' carefree confidence confounded Allyne, but she clearly recognized Bertha's motive.

Miss Collins had desired an invitation to Mrs. Adelia Alston's kettledrum and made calculated employ of Allyne to win Miss Halloran's favor. Yet Allyne couldn't resent Bertha for making such use of her. Now acquainted with Lillis, Allyne had no further use for Miss Collins of Peoria.

Miss Collins fought to contain her stretching smile as she bid her guests good afternoon. Basking in the success of her enterprise, Bertha sauntered to the railing, her gaze lost where the lake met the horizon beyond the tips of Michigan's Upper and Lower Peninsulas.

Seeing Lillis had given her a delightful thrill, though Anne Kearney had decidedly mitigated the effect. Being nice to Anne had been difficult, but Bertha forgave Lillis the encumbrance when she forgot her old friend for the shiny new object from New York. Anne had been as neglected as Bertha by Misses Halloran and Vandermeer, but at least Bertha had an invitation to Mrs. Alston's kettledrum to show for it.

And Lillis would no doubt show Bertha gratitude for introducing Miss Vandermeer. Bertha repressed her jealous inclinations. Of course Lillis had taken to Allyne – she had always loved new people. Lillis would golf with her and make a fuss over her at social gatherings and devote herself to the eastern girl's entertainment, but at summer's end Miss Vandermeer would return to New York and Lillis would remember that she had Bertha to thank for her summer friendship.

The more she admired Miss Vandermeer, the more impressed Lillis must be by Bertha's judgment of character and social promise. No doubt she would invite Bertha to spend another weekend with her in Chicago. They would attend a society ball, or one of the younger Halloran's debuts, or perhaps visit the theater. Bertha could see them now, promenading up Michigan Avenue in an open victoria, the most admired ladies in all of Illinois.

Five

"Another capital convention," Merit Jones declared, waddling between his half of the second wardrobe and the open portmanteau at his bed's foot. "Of course it's real easy for the likes of Smith and Cooper to lord their earnings over the rest of us. My territory is rural – all humble farmers. Give me the north shore of Chicago and I'll show you earnings! Am I right?

"Say – why aren't you packing? Oh, that's right – you're staying through the weekend. It's a right pretty place, this island, but I don't envy you. This room's been downright uncomfortable in the evenings, with that sun. And of course I miss my Bessie. I wait all year for a spell away from Bessie and the little ones, but by about now I'm mighty lonesome for them. Well, Mr. Drury," Mr. Jones snapped the portmanteau shut and approached with extended hand, which Del promptly rose from his chair to shake. "I hope you enjoy this weekend."

"Thank you," Del murmured. "Safe journey."

"Oh," Merit Jones paused just before reaching the door. "I picked up your mail – two letters for you, on the table there. Good luck to you, Drury."

"And to you, Mr. Jones."

Del's muscles contracted—like a cat just before it pounces upon its prey—as he watched the door close behind Merit Jones's broad back. The latch's fastening click acted upon Del like a starter's gun; he leapt from his chair and nearly fell upon the letters. He had torn open one envelope, but hesitated before withdrawing its contents.

Surely this was too good to be true? Ten minutes ago Del had watched Merit Jones pack his bag with hopeless sense of fate's cruelties. That was his destiny – to be an insurance salesman with nothing more to look forward to than the Western Life Insurance agents' annual convention. His college friends toured Europe; Del would solicit a larger territory of rural Indiana. His childhood friends practiced law or owned banks but spent their summers at some pleasant watering spot; Del could follow them and try to sell their acquaintances life insurance policies. Del had almost resigned himself to this future and yet his fickle resolve wavered with the arrival of two letters.

With pounding heart and ringing ears, Del withdrew the envelope's contents: a letter, and a check. *Scribner's* had accepted his essay on the modern sporting man – it would be published in their August issue. And they included a check for twenty-five dollars.

Bolstered by this small success, Del took more care with his second envelope. Breaking its seal with his letter opener, he thrilled to see the missive from *Harper's*. Their check for his short story about an Indiana boy attempting to navigate New York society was far more substantial; *Harper's* planned to publish the work in installments from

September through November and requested he send them a Christmas-themed story for their December issue.

Del drifted about the room in dazed, euphoric state. For three years, he had submitted essays and stories and poems to every magazine in the country. Now—when he had finally determined to forsake his literary aspirations—he had two acceptances in the same day! This was assuredly Divine intervention – the good Lord saving him from a life of drudgery just as he had abandoned all hope!

The checks were no fortune, but they provided the necessary finances to stay at Grand Hotel all summer if he chose. The insurance agent still lurking within him cautioned Del against this action. He should save his money, for he had precious little of it left. And yet – was not this gift from God a sign that he should pursue his literary ambitions? Now that they had finally accepted a submission from him, *Harper's* and *Scribner's* would give more consideration to his future submissions. And where better—at this crucial moment—would Del find inspiration for good dramatic prose than this prestigious, fashionable island?

Del devoted far more time deliberating upon the best method of inspiring Allyne Vandermeer's acknowledgment than he gave to his future with the Western Life Insurance Company. Within an hour of receiving the two acceptance letters, Del had secured a room at the eastern end of the long central hall, reserving it through the end of August. He had dispatched his resignation letter and a brief note to his mother apprising her of his change in circumstance. In that one hour he had completed a full metamorphosis from insurance agent to writer. Those bleak days of compromised honor were so far behind him that Del scarce recalled their particular feelings of desperation and pragmatic resolve. He was buoyed by hope – drunk with small successes that confirmed his preconceived belief in his talent as a writer. In short, Del was quick to embrace his dearest desire when it suddenly manifested in the form of two checks.

Obtaining Allyne Vandermeer's acknowledgment was a far more complex matter requiring many hours of pondering. If she had recognized him, then she now deliberately snubbed him and he should not push himself upon her. Yet Del had never been unkind to Miss Vandermeer and he still corresponded amicably with her cousin. Del had great capacity for perception; he sensed emotion in others and often surmised its cause – this talent made his fictional characters so compelling. He was fairly certain Miss Vandermeer had merely been distracted when their paths had crossed and would welcome reunion with an old acquaintance. But what if her distraction persisted and she never saw him? And would she really welcome his reappearance if she did see him? They had not been particularly friendly when he lived in New York – cordial, but not friendly.

After weighing the dilemma over the next few days, Del sprang into action that cool, misty morning. He knew there was a reason he had packed his old Princeton sweater. Donning the orange and black garment, Del navigated the long hall and sloping staircase and stepped briskly through the parlor to the front porch. Rain prevented him from cycling or hiking, but Del could not let a day lapse without some form of physical exertion. He believed in regular exercise to maintain a body's ideal weight and muscular definition. Today, briskly strolling upon the world's longest front porch would have to suffice. And Miss Vandermeer would notice the sweater when he passed her rocking chair.

Miss Vandermeer's gaze drifted to the picturesque red and white lighthouse upon the tip of Round Island—barely conscious of Bertha's ramblings from the neighboring rocking chair—and wondered if Lillis' family owned a suitable yacht. She wanted to explore the surrounding islands, to sail past the two peninsula points into the sinking sunset... If Miss Halloran did not have access to a yacht, Allyne would acquire her own. Surely one of these cottagers would sell if offered enough money; Allyne had been raised upon the comforting notion that enough money devoted to an issue always resolved it in her favor.

A figure in garish orange and black sweater briefly obstructed Allyne's view of the lighthouse. Her cousin William had a sweater just like it . . . Could Grand Hotel have attracted a Princeton man? Allyne's eyes followed his retreating figure; admittedly he possessed a fine figure, which the sweater displayed far better than any morning coat or blazer. Yet no glimmer of recognition occurred to her until he had turned at the porch end to retrace his steps. She had seen him before – back home, though she couldn't recall where. How could she forget the name of a man so handsome? She knew him. He went to Princeton, William's friend – Del something. That was it.

"Mr.—" she rose to her feet as their eyes met. "You must think me most ill-mannered, but I cannot recall your last name! But of course I recognize William's dear friend, Del."

"Drury," he bowed. "Though I'd prefer for you to forget again and call me 'Del'."

"Only if you'll call me Allyne," she returned.

A slight cough recalled Bertha's presence to Allyne.

"May I present Miss Bertha Collins?" Allyne offered the introduction. "Of Peoria. Mr. Drury—Del—was at Princeton with my cousin William."

"It's a pleasure to meet you, Miss Collins," Del bowed as Bertha emphatically agreed.

His searching eyes returned to Allyne, as though he expected a full explanation of her unrefined companion's presence.

"What brings you to Mackinac Island?" Allyne asked before he could.

"You do know that this is the Midwest's premier summer resort? And that I'm from Indiana?"

His hazel eyes crinkled with his teasing tone, but Allyne recognized his reluctance to provide a ready and truthful answer.

"Who are you here with?" she pressed.

"No one," Del shrugged, his grin fading. "I thought Mackinac would be quiet enough to write by day and lively enough to give respite in the evenings."

"Write?" Allyne was intrigued. "What do you write? Poetry or prose?"

"Oh, a little of everything. I have an essay coming out in *Scribner's* next month and *Harper's* will be publishing a short story of mine in the fall. This place rather inspires me to write a novel."

"A writer..." Allyne drawled. "You must have gone to class far more than William."

"Not at all; I was just smarter going in. But what of you, Allyne? You're not from Indiana."

"No," she let her glance drift back to the lighthouse. "I'm here with my grandmothers."

"Both of them?" Del's expression exuded sympathy.

"Yes, but after a year in Europe together I'm quite used to them."

"From Europe to Michigan?"

"I've always wanted to see the west."

"You'd have to hop a few states over for that."

"Well, I just might. I've heard California is beautiful."

"Yes, I've heard the same," Del played along like a gentleman; he must know by now that she fled something back in New York, but politely refrained from further inquiries in that line.

"Will you dine with us Saturday?" Allyne invited impulsively.

She did not believe Del or her grandmothers would benefit much from the other's company, but the thought of poor Del dining at a solitary table invoked her tender sympathies.

"It would be my greatest pleasure," Del accepted.

"Lovely – we'll meet you at eight o'clock just outside the dining room's entrance."

"I look forward to it," Del bowed in farewell before resuming his brisk stroll up the porch.

"Was he a beau of yours back in New York?"

Allyne turned with a start at the question; she had completely forgotten Bertha's presence for a few minutes.

"Don't be silly," her lofty tone cowed Bertha, but only for a moment.

"He's very handsome – so tall, with rather a regal bearing. His hair was an enviable chestnut color. His nature was charming, affable..."

After such praise for Del Drury, Allyne expected Miss Collins to express her desire to have him for her beau.

"Do you think Lillis would like him?" Bertha asked instead.

Allyne looked forward to this venture, though not quite to the degree of Miss Collins. Bertha's round cheeks flushed avidly and her eyes gleamed in eager anticipation of the afternoon's delights. Or perhaps it was merely the thought of being in Lillis' presence that inspired her expression. Perhaps Bertha was unaware that kettledrums had fallen out of fashion years ago, or perhaps they were still popular in the Middle West. Allyne didn't care to sample the food or see the house or for the chance to expand her social network; she went to observe the Hallorans.

"Pine Bluff," Bertha spoke the name with reverence as their victoria transported them the short distance up West Bluff Road. "Isn't it grand? They say it's the finest cottage on the whole island. Can you imagine calling a home that large a 'cottage?' It's as big as my house in Peoria!"

"You've obviously never been to Newport," Allyne drawled. "Our cottage there is thrice as large."

Bertha was sufficiently cowed, but Allyne would never admit that Pine Bluff had thrice the charm of the rambling, old Newport cottage Grandmother Vandermeer loved more than all her children and grandchildren, (though not quite so much as her cocker spaniel). Pine Bluff looked like a home. A hammock stretched between pillars at the rounded eastern end of the gracious, wraparound front porch. Each tower, bay window and small covered balcony seemed personally designed for the home's occupants – nothing else could explain its whimsical lack of uniformity. Pink and purple petunias spilled from baskets along the porch and balcony railings, their colors eclipsed only by the massive American flag furling from its pillar-mounted pole. A little girl and even younger boy in matching straw boaters leaned over the central balcony railing to observe the arriving guests. Yes – Pine Bluff was grand, but not for the reasons Bertha valued.

The soft din Allyne detected when stepping down from the carriage block intensified to full cacophony at the top of the porch steps. Feminine shrieks and laughter played against a steady tempo from... yes, they had a drum!

A few couples lounged upon the wicker sofas and rocking chairs beneath the hanging ferns and Chinese lanterns descending from the porch ceiling. The majority of guests, however, congregated in the large parlor. The exquisite woodwork on the staircase, wainscoting, thick paneling, and ornate ceiling predominated over the plush furnishings, colorful cushions and vases of fresh flowers. Surrounded by every luxury, Allyne still felt herself in a rustic northern cabin.

Guests crowded around the cluster of settees and chairs before the broad fireplace, where a woman in splendid Indian headdress beat a mesmeric rhythm upon an antique drum.

"Allyne! Bertha!" Lillis strode toward them with extended hands and returned to the circle around her aunt with the new arrivals in tow.

"I come with offerings!" Lillis called over the drumbeat. "May I present Miss Allyne Vandermeer of New York and Miss Bertha Collins of Peoria to their warrior princess, chieftain and hostess, Mrs. Alston."

Adelia Alston was the most beautiful woman Allyne had ever seen. The distinct, yet delicate lines of her face and porcelain skin bore a strong resemblance to her niece, Lillis, but Adelia's coloring enhanced the dramatic beauty of these features. Her skin was a glowing alabaster surrounded by thick, auburn hair. Her face, a lily, accentuated by thin, arched brows and thick black lashes. The mass of feathered headdress and her perch over the drum could not detract from her elegance. And yet Allyne had never beheld a hostess so . . . wild. Mrs. Alston beat upon that drum with such carefree confidence; she sought no one's approval. Allyne had never witnessed a lady's actions dictated only by her whim at a social gathering. Mrs. Alston had the knack of the perfect hostess who knows her guests will only have as much fun as the lady of the house.

"And their Chippewa names?" Mrs. Alston asked with raised brows.

"Raven Hair and Long Neck," Lillis promptly replied.

"So pleased to meet you, R-a-a-ven Hair and Looonnng

Neck," Mrs. Alston beat the drums in cadence with her exaggerated pronunciations.

Allyne felt the color rush from her chin to her hairline; she had always been self-conscious about her neck. Milton said it resembled a swan, but Josie had teased her about its length mercilessly since childhood. Long Neck might be a nicer moniker than Black Swan, but Allyne resented it no less.

"I welcome you to my table and home," Mrs. Alston spoke with the solemnity of an Indian chief receiving prisoners before her blazing, victorious bonfire.

Suddenly Allyne felt grateful for the welcome. Glancing at the smiling faces on either side of her, at the gleaming wood-carved mantel behind Mrs. Alston and the glistening Straits beyond the front windows, Allyne finally felt she had an anchor to this island. So accustomed to staying at one of her own houses or that of a friend, her recent weeks at Grand Hotel had produced the sensation of floating – of weightless, desultory drifting. Even in the European capitals, Allyne had always been welcome in someone's home. And now she was again, here on Mackinac Island. The Hallorans were new money – more upstart than the Van Buhlers. They were Irish! And likely Papists! And yet Allyne was glad to be welcomed into their realm.

Lillis led Allyne and Bertha to the refreshment table. Allyne poured herself a cup of coffee and selected anything incorporating chocolate from the ample spread. Anne Kearney introduced Olivia Wheeler, whose family's original Annex cottage was next to the old Eating House.

"I miss the Wacheo," Lillis lamented.

"The what?" Allyne frowned.

"The old Eating House," Miss Wheeler explained. "None of the original cottages had kitchens. We took all of our meals at the Wacheo."

"I don't miss it," a buxom blonde woman in lovely apricot dress declared. "Our Anna is a far better cook and it was rather tiresome walking there for every meal."

"Mother, may I present Miss Allyne Vandermeer?" Lillis made the introduction.

"I thought this was Long Neck?" Mrs. Halloran's eyes twinkled with mischievous delight.

Allyne envied Lillis for having such a mother. She had never looked upon faces that exhibited such mutual affection as Mrs. Halloran and Lillis. Their look exuded love and shared secrets, mirth and candor. Allyne's mother had died twelve hours after birthing her; she had never shared such a glance with either of her grandmothers and had shared such few looks with her father she could not recall the color of his eyes. Nor had she ever enjoyed such companionable banter with her relations as Lillis and her mother shared with their extended family.

In the hour they lingered, Allyne met nearly all of the Hallorans and most of Lillis' friends. (Bertha had longed to stay on, but it wasn't fashionable to remain more than an hour at a kettledrum.) Anne Kearney had offered a brief history of each new acquaintance: Cousin Alva's father had more money than his two brothers and father combined, though not so much as his sister's husband. Paddy Halloran—the family patriarch—was probably drunk with Uncle Brennan out on the yacht, *Northern*

Spirit – yes, the pun was intentional. And yes, the family sailed to Mass each Sunday, either on *Northern Spirit* or Lillis' father's equally impressive *Northern Splendor*. No, Uncle Brennan didn't have a yacht; he didn't even own his own cottage, but assumes he'll inherit Lakeview Cottage since his siblings each have their own finer dwellings.

Allyne thought Anne Kearney's candid discussion of money and wealth vulgar. Back home all of these factors would be known, but never mentioned. Though as she was ill-acquainted with Midwestern society and less so of these Mackinac cottagers, Allyne did appreciate Miss Kearney's vulgarity.

Del retreated to his room, writing witty sketches of Miss Vandermeer and Miss Collins. The lily and dandelion, he named them – tall, elegant fragility beside sturdy, striving tenacity. What did Allyne flee? Del's realist practicality subdued fantastic speculation; only a broken engagement or some other romantic scandal could have induced Miss Vandermeer's Midwestern seclusion. More than her pride must have suffered for a year abroad to be insufficient to restore her confidence. And Miss Collins – what did she seek? Social elevation? An advantageous marriage?

When the humid air made his paper as limp as his thoughts, Del set his pen aside. At least it had stopped raining. The porch stroll had not been strenuous enough to exercise his restless muscles. The ground might be too damp for a bicycle, but he could at least walk through the woods.

Rain-enhanced aromas of cedar and pine intoxicated Del as he traversed the sloping woods bordering Grand Hotel's front lawn. Lethargic thoughts were impossible amidst such crisp environment. The fresh, lake-scented air made his step brisker and filled him with purpose. Del felt he could do anything in air so pure and invigorating; he would write a novel this summer – a masterpiece!

The soft, rhythmic splash of waves breaking upon stones drew Del toward the island's southwestern shore. The water mirrored the pewter sky, but even shades of gray were beautiful on Mackinac Island. A strip of hazy blue hovered over the Lake Michigan horizon, promising a sunny finish to the day. And—as if today hadn't been blessed enough—a certain elegant lady stood just twenty yards down the beach, looking wistfully at that line of blue sky. She didn't acknowledge Del's approach until he skipped a stone through her gaze's path.

"Impressive," she declared as his stone sank after its sixth skip. "I've only ever managed five skips."

Did she seek a tutorial? Del hoped, but thought it best not to ask.

"I confess, that was my intention – to impress you by any means possible in hope of recognition."

"I knew I'd seen you before!" she cried, and her face transformed with her smile from severely beautiful to irresistibly adorable; she looked a cool thirty-four with sober expression, but just now she couldn't be more than nineteen. "In Indianapolis – that is where I've seen you?"

"Yes–I believe our paths crossed at some holiday festivity hosted by my mother and stepfather, Otis Holderson."

"Yes, I remember," she nodded, still smiling. "Amaryllis Holderson, formerly Mrs. Delbert Drury. You're the namesake – her son."

Del bowed in acknowledgement, "At your service, Mrs. Pruett."

"My Christian name is Priscilla, though my friends call me 'Prissy'."

"Priscilla is a beautiful name," Del murmured, lost in her brilliantly blue eyes.

She was suddenly shy, her cheeks flushing as her sweeping lashes hid her eyes.

"I'm surprised we haven't met since the holidays," her smooth tone betrayed no emotion. "Have you been away from Indianapolis?"

"Yes, I've been traveling."

Priscilla noticed the color rise in his face, but was too refined to acknowledge his brief display of discomfort. She seemed relieved for some reason – at least the two narrow furrows across her forehead evaporated as she lifted her gaze once more to meet his.

"What brings you to Mackinac Island, Mr. Drury?"

"I thought it the ideal place to work on my next novel," Del spoke as if his "next" followed at least a dozen prior published works.

"Are you a writer?" Priscilla's intrigued look sent Del's spirits soaring. "Surely it should be all over town that Mrs. Holderson's son is a famed author?"

She teased him now – how her eyes twinkled in challenge! He wanted to tackle her to the stones and—

"I'm a writer," Del stepped closer until she had to tilt her graceful chin back to meet his eyes. "Not an author. I've been published in *Scribner's* and *Harper's*," he spoke in casual tone, as if these recent achievements were old hat. "But I've lately been inspired to pen a novel."

"What most inspires you?" she asked archly. "The beautiful landscape or the people you've observed?"

"Both."

"I hope you won't put me in your novel," Priscilla murmured as she knelt to select a thin, flat stone from the beach.

"Very good," Del offered for her five skips. "And of course you'll be in my novel – as its beautiful heroine."

"Not if you expect your novel to succeed," she scoffed, flubbing another fat stone that plunked beneath the water after only two skips. "I'm far too boring for fiction."

"No one with a face like yours could lead a boring life."

"My," Priscilla took a step back from him, her eyes wary, yet alert. "You are a romantic."

"I dare anyone not to be romantic on this fairy island."

"You're too divine," she murmured, hiding her smile as she turned to stroll up the beach.

Del followed her through the cedars, matching her languid stride up the shore road.

"I'm here with my family," she spoke when they reached the wooded path leading back to the hotel.

"Yes," Del nodded. "I saw your children in the carriages that day; they were as beautiful as their mother. And your mother is here, as well?"

"My mother?" Priscilla frowned. "Oh – in the carriage. That was Mrs. Polly Easton, or maybe Mrs. Webb . . . My mother remains in Indianapolis with my brother and his family."

Her eyes flitted to his, seemingly granting permission to ignore all existence of her husband. *She desires me,* Del perceived with an exuberant jolt. She's on the cusp of abandonment – of relinquishing every virtue and scruple formerly governing her conduct. Some passion drove her. Del wasn't so egotistical as to assume responsibility for her passion. He merely recognized that something inspired that determined gleam in her eyes.

"I love this island," Priscilla's soft voice drew him closer, luring him into her confidence. "The fresh air invigorates me; the views take my breath away. I'm intoxicated with fairies' fancies and a sky full of wishing stars. But its most appealing aspects lie in their contrast to my real life in Indianapolis."

"In what way?" Del asked, and suddenly Priscilla's elegant mask rose over her formerly candid beauty; she wanted him to appreciate her circumstance without revealing the details of its cause. Priscilla rather enjoyed her aura of mystery; Del realized the futility of pressing her further.

"Are you a friend, Mr. Drury?" she asked softly.

"Only if you'll call me 'Del'."

"But you'll never call me 'Prissy'."

"No," he spoke through lips pressed to her smooth cheek. "Priscilla – my fairy queen."

Her kiss was so sweet, her embrace so rousing; Del feared he would lose himself in her arms. Pausing at the woods edge—a sumptuous nymph in her delicate, white lawn dress—Priscilla stole a last kiss from his infatuated lips.

"I shall always treasure this afternoon," she declared, her eyes earnest as she lifted his hands in firm clasp.

"Priscilla," Del retained her left hand, holding her back from flight. "This wasn't our only fine afternoon. We'll have many more before summer's end."

"Will we?" she smiled sadly, yet with bravely upturned jaw.

"Oh, yes," Del assured her.

He stood at the woods' edge, concealed among the cedars, watching Priscilla's children flock to her from the lawn. Her forced cheer and bravado could not erase the impression of repressed fury Del detected behind her smooth veneer. Priscilla Pruett was an angry woman – her emotion made her reckless. Del realized he could easily have her, just as he recognized she was worth the effort to win.

Six

"I asked for my brassie," Allyne frowned upon Georgie Halloran – or was this his brother, Tommy? She couldn't tell Lillis' young cousins apart.

Their father, Brennan, was the family's black sheep. He may not own his own cottage or yacht, he may be fonder of drinking Halloran's Fine Whiskey than promoting its sale, but Brennan had thus far sired more Hallorans to carry on the family name than any of his siblings. Even in a clan as prosperous as these Hallorans, the poorest member had the most children to support. His eldest son seemed on course to follow in his father's disappointing footsteps, the verdict was still out on his youngest son and daughter, but Brennan's second and third sons seemed earnestly industrious. Lillis said they traversed this little five-hole meadow course every day in hope of a caddy commission. Yet Allyne thought Tommy—or was it Georgie?—would earn a better tip if he bothered to hand her the club she had requested.

"The hole's only fifty yards out," the boy protested.

"A brassie would send you into that tall grass and you'd lose another ball," Lillis agreed.

"And I'm not going in that grass after it," Tommy declared.

"Here," Lillis handed her an iron. "Use my mashie."

"But I can't hit it as far as you!" Allyne protested.

"At least use your spoon," Tommy held out the higher loft wood hopefully.

Allyne took his advice and crowed triumphantly when her ball rolled up to the green's edge.

"I should listen to you more often, Georgie," Allyne offered him fond smile.

"It's Tommy – and yes, you should," the boy agreed, readjusting his tweed cap at jaunty, confident angle.

"What do you recommend for my next club?" she asked as they strolled down the sloping fairway. "My jigger?"

"I think it's safest to putt from there," Tommy advised.

Allyne conceded that her approach shots had been abysmal today.

"Well done!" Lillis congratulated Allyne for finally winning a hole.

"Thanks," Allyne beamed. "I haven't golfed in two years."

"I only learned to golf two years ago," Lillis grinned.

"You're very good."

"Well, I play nearly every day on Mackinac. Golf is a game of long odds – your only hope of winning is to play so often you have a good shot among a profusion of attempts. But why have you forsaken this glorious game for two whole years?"

"I was abroad," Allyne murmured evasively. "We left in May, so I missed last summer."

"Where did you go?"

"Everywhere," Allyne shrugged.

"Have you seen Rothenburg and the castles in Bavaria?" Lillis asked eagerly.

"No," Allyne flushed, anticipating her companion's next words.

"So – not everywhere?" Lillis' grin was infectious; it mocked Allyne's pompous tone, but forgave her with good-natured grace and wry sense of humor.

"I've only been twice," Lillis offered as they approached the fifth tee. "With Mother just before my debut. We visited great aunts and uncles and cousins back in the homeland – Ireland, I mean; County Galway. Then of course it was on to Paris for wardrobe replenishment in September. And Mother was sweet enough to succumb to my Bavarian whim for two glorious weeks of October before sailing home."

"I've never been to Ireland or Bavaria," Allyne acknowledged. "What of the other time – where else did you visit?"

"Oh, it was a proper tour. Kitty was fifteen, I was eleven and Patrick only four. We tried Paris in early spring, Vienna in late spring, then Venice, Florence, Rome, Aix, Geneva and St. Moritz; September in Ireland and then home."

"St. Moritz is one of my favorite places," Allyne declared, smiling as she took the brassie Tommy offered.

They played out the last hole, each with equal strife to triumph. Allyne missed her putt and surrendered the hole to Lillis by a stroke. Tommy and Georgie were paid their fee; Allyne offered Tommy five additional dollars to see her golf bag returned to Grand Hotel.

"You must be famished – I am," Lillis spoke as they ambled up the dusty Annex road, carefully circumventing horse droppings in varying degrees of decomposition. "Join me for luncheon on the veranda? Anna will have put sandwiches out, and lemonade."

Allyne impulsively accepted the invitation and devoured two chicken salad, one egg salad, and one cucumber sandwich whilst rocking on the glider beside Lillis. The view from Sunset Cottage's west veranda was unobstructed and unrivaled on the island. The cottage perched on the bluff top, presiding over gracious lawn sloping toward the treetops clinging to the cliffs below. The sea—or rather, the lake—glistened like a bed of yellow diamonds in the afternoon sunlight. Allyne marveled at the sky's vastness here, in this remote, austerely beautiful spec of the globe.

Alas, Halloran verandas were not made for reverence or reflection – or any singular pursuit. Within ten minutes of their arrival, Lillis' brother Patrick fell upon the sandwich tray; cousin Alva and her younger brothers waited their turn with much banter and laughter.

"And then our hansom driver said, 'Jesus, Mary and Joseph!'" Lillis spoke with strong Irish brogue. "And Mama and Papa called 'Yes?'"

They all burst out laughing. Allyne thought it exceedingly funny that Lillis' Irish parents claimed the names Mary and Joseph. The Hallorans answered Allyne's idle wonder of what her chambermaid, cook and kitchen maids would look like with money. They were jolly – as heathen in daily practice as they were devout in traditional adherence. Her grandmothers considered Catholics a primitive species, but Allyne thought their religion far more compatible with daily life. Protestants were severely demanding; Catholics possessed confidence of complete absolution and enjoyed life between confessions. Lillis' Catholicism was prevalent in this sense – she lived for the moment, with complete faith of divine forgiveness later.

"Will you attend our lawn party for St. Anne's?" Lillis asked, sliding closer to Allyne on the glider to make room for Alva as the younger boys galloped down the veranda and across the lawn.

"St. Anne's?" Allyne inquired.

"July 26 is the feast day of St. Anne," Alva informed her.

"We're hosting an ice cream festival here at Sunset Cottage," Lillis explained. "All proceeds will be donated to St. Anne's. I can't recall for what this year... I believe they have a new altar, and pews... perhaps the roof? At any rate, the Hallorans host a festival on St. Anne's Feast Day every summer to raise funds for the church and parish. We'll have lawn games and thirteen ice cream flavors to sample. Say you'll come?"

"I wouldn't miss it," Allyne promised.

"I suppose you'll come with Bertha?" Lillis sighed.

"Miss Collins?" Allyne asked in derisive tone for the subject. "Of course I would accompany her were she also afforded an invitation, but I am perfectly content to come on my own accord."

"Our ice cream festival is for the church; we don't discriminate – anyone on the island is welcome to attend. But Mother wishes to host you and your grandmothers for Sunday dinner. Are you available this weekend?"

"Yes," Allyne nodded.

"But let's golf again before then!" Lillis implored as she refilled their lemonade glasses.

"Of course – to golf and everything. I've few other acquaintances on the island, and am very glad to have met you. And I fully appreciate your wish to be free of Miss Collins, but were you not friends in Chicago?"

"Hardly," Lillis' laughter had the tinkling quality of champagne-filled crystal. "We were at Rosewood Seminary together, but did not know each other socially, Bertha being from Peoria. It was rather a surprise to discover her here on Mackinac."

"She is surprising," Allyne agreed before settling their next tee time.

In her enchantment of Annex cottages peeking demurely from behind boxwood or hydrangea hedges, nestled among the trees like so many colorful treasures in a cedar chest, Allyne forgot about Bertha Collins on her walk back to Grand Hotel.

Waiting in restless vigil upon parlor settee with prime view of the front doors, Bertha Collins had not forgotten Allyne in all the hours the latter had spent with Lillis. She was slightly mollified by rereading the *Resorter's Gazette* account of Mrs. Alston's kettledrum – particularly the lines mentioning her:

Miss Vandermeer arrived with Miss Bertha Collins of Peoria. Miss Collins and her grandmother are also guests at Grand Hotel.

Of course this snippet was not so satisfying as the two paragraphs describing the porch tea Bertha had hosted for Miss Vandermeer, but she was glad to be mentioned again. Lillis' name was mentioned at least once in every issue; Bertha could not compete with Lillis, but she hoped to be mentioned at least as often as Anne Kearney.

"Good gracious, how long can it take to play a round of golf?" Bertha muttered when the next glance upon her watch reminded her that she had perched upon this settee for two and a half hours.

Bertha rose, casting about for a more comfortable chair, when Allyne's tall, willowy figure finally floated up the porch steps and through the front doors.

"Miss Vandermeer," Bertha called twice before Allyne noticed her.

"Oh – good afternoon, Miss Collins. I'm just returning to my room."

"As am I," Bertha declared, leaving the lady no polite manner of evading her company as she climbed the stairs at Allyne's side. "How did your golf outing fare?"

"Lillis beat me four out of five holes, but it felt good to play again."

Five holes? Bertha had assumed they played the course at least twice; Allyne had been gone for hours!

"Did she invite you to Sunset Cottage?" Bertha blurted the question.

"Oh, yes," Allyne nodded as Bertha struggled to keep up with her long-legged stride down the west hall. "A lovely place – its west veranda must have the best view on the island."

"You had luncheon there?" Bertha was determined to extract every enviable detail of Lillis' afternoon.

"Just sandwiches and lemonade on the veranda," Allyne spoke as they climbed the stairs to the third floor. "Alva and some of the younger cousins joined us. They're such a jolly lot, the Hallorans. And isn't it too funny that her parents are named Mary and Joseph?"

Bertha forced a laugh, hoping her sudden swell of resentment did not show upon her face. She had not known Mrs. Halloran's Christian name. It wasn't fair that Allyne had been acquainted with Lillis for only two weeks, yet had knowledge of her that Bertha lacked!

"I thought your room was at the east end?" Allyne paused five yards up the west hall.

"Oh," Bertha flushed. "Yes – of course. Good afternoon."

She spun on her heel, hoping Miss Vandermeer had not noticed the color rising to her cheeks. Bertha had known Allyne would admire Lillis, but she had not anticipated the seeming degree of Lillis' reciprocal sentiment. Golf was to blame; no doubt Allyne would go out with Lillis again – countless hours alone on the links to become better acquainted, to foster friendship and inspire admiration. Bertha's first thought was how to inflict a wrist or ankle sprain upon Allyne that would look accidental. She briefly considered golf lessons, but knew she could not progress quickly enough to infiltrate Lillis' and Allyne's golf outings this summer.

Delaying the confrontation with her grandmother's tired, wary eyes, Bertha paced before their door at the east end of the third floor hall. Perhaps she had read too much into Miss Vandermeer's lightly uttered words this afternoon. Thus far she had shared Allyne's every interaction with Lillis. And the only reason she had been excluded from their meeting today was her lack of golfing prowess. It wasn't that they didn't want Bertha's presence, but they had accepted the reason for her absence a little too complacently. Yet they had only golfed once – today. Lillis had invited both her and Allyne to the St. Anne's ice cream social next Wednesday. Allyne wouldn't see her before then, unless Lillis attended the hotel's Saturday ball. Bertha was silly to worry. Just the same, she intended to keep more careful watch of Miss Vandermeer's activities.

Franklin Pruett stood at the porch railing, smiling fondly upon Emmeline and Francis playing on the vast lawn below. Monty and Gil slouched in the shadows at the woods' edge, but he had faith in his eldest sons to look after their younger brother and sister. Priscilla never had a nanny in the house; she hadn't trusted anyone to raise their children better than she could. They were the brightest, handsomest children he knew – if not a little too smart for their own good.

Letting his gaze drift over the treetops to the brilliantly blue water, Franklin took a breath of the fresh, crisp air and let a contented sigh escape. What a relief to be five hundred miles away from Ethel's needy pleas and Amos King's shotgun!

How had he let things come to such a pass? Keeping a mistress whilst dallying with a colleague's wife? Amos and Florence King had attended his fifteenth wedding anniversary ball in June. Two days later, Ethel had confronted poor Florence outside the town's finest, most frequented dry goods emporium; everyone in Indianapolis society had the news by five o'clock.

"How could you be so reckless?" Priscilla had cried with more passion than she had exhibited for him in years – which was precisely why he had been so reckless.

Franklin strolled above the jangling tack and plodding hooves as the beautiful draft horses pulled a shining, maroon Grand Hotel carriage to the foot of the porch steps. The young family alighting from this stately equipage drew his attention; Franklin lingered at the porch railing to better observe them.

What a family! All handsome, with bright eyes and expectantly upturned faces. Three children—their soft, curly hair flouncing under matching boaters—held hands as they followed their parents up the steps. Their mother was a vision – crowned by mass of golden curls, adorned with rosy lips and cheeks, molded in the shape of a perfect hourglass. Franklin didn't envy her husband for her face or figure, but for the radiant smile she flashed upon him as he led her into the parlor. That smile showed gratitude, pride and love for the man she bestowed it upon. Priscilla hadn't looked upon him with such a smile in at least seven years.

She certainly wasn't smiling now, as she stepped out to the porch. After an over-the-shoulder glance to the family he had been observing, Priscilla's eyes returned to his. She looked especially pretty today, an uncharacteristic flush warming her face – or at least it had been warm before alighting upon him.

"I thought you were watching Emmeline and Francis?" she reproached him.

"I was observing them play just now, but I've put Monty and Gil in charge of their care for the next hour or so."

She signaled her indifference to his ulterior plans by the slightest shrug of her narrow shoulders.

"I'm meeting Mr. Maier this afternoon, to inspect the cottage. I don't suppose—"

"I'm going for a walk," Priscilla cut him off, saving herself from answering his question by stopping its utterance.

"I'll see you at dinner, then," he bowed to her already retreating figure.

"Why didn't you tell me about Adelia Halloran?" Iva sprang the question upon her husband in pragmatic tone as he swept the front porch after breakfast.

Elliott swept the broom across the freshly painted floorboards a few more times to compose himself before meeting his wife's powder blue eyes. Clad in tailored morning suit with hat perched over her gray-blonde hair and gloves in hand, Iva was clearly on her way out for some errand. Did she broach the topic with such limited time for explanation because she anticipated a simple, benign response?

"What about Miss Ha – Mrs. Alston?" he adopted a blank, innocent expression.

"She was still Miss Halloran when you asked her to marry you, I believe?" Iva's eyes narrowed as she tugged her kid gloves more firmly over her fingers. "That might have been nice to mention before encouraging me to accept the invitation to her kettledrum."

"I didn't want to burden you; it was all so long ago, it means nothing to me."

"It obviously means something, or you would have burdened me."

The sound of approaching hooves silenced Elliott and Iva. They watched the dark-haired, debonair gentleman dismount from his thoroughbred, loop his reins through the hitching post and step through the front gate. Elliott's reluctance to discuss Adelia with Iva was so great that he welcomed the appearance of the man to whom he must relinquish Mapleview.

"Mr. Pruett," Elliott descended the porch steps to shake the man's hand. "May I introduce Mrs. Maier?"

Pruett bowed to Iva.

"It's nice to meet you, Mr. Pruett. Please forgive my abrupt departure? I'm walking into town for groceries with Mrs. Pendleton and some other neighbors. We're to meet at eleven-thirty by the old Eating House."

"Of course," Pruett bowed again as Iva floated up the walk and through the front gate.

"A lovely lady," Pruett offered.

"Thank you," Elliott nodded. "Shall we walk through the cottage?"

Elliott strove to retain a neutral façade as he led Franklin Pruett through the house his father had built. He loathed the appraising manner with which Pruett regarded the familiar rooms. Pruett saw faded walls and rustic, old furnishings; Elliott saw his brother, Peter—forever eight years old in his memory—stretched on the far twin bed with a book held up to his nose. Pruett saw a cluttered parlor, gloomy beneath a wood-paneled ceiling, surrounded by wood-paneled walls; Elliott saw his mother presiding over a teapot from the couch, her proud expression drawing the admiring eye of every lady in the room. Pruett saw a lovely bedroom for his daughter; Elliott saw his sister Laura curled upon the window seat cushion, her long, blonde hair dancing with the lace curtains in the west breeze. Yet when Pruett took the offered rocking chair on the veranda's southwest corner, his gaze aligned with Elliott's in appreciation of their view. Over the hydrangea hedge, between the two Halloran cottages across the boulevard, the Straits' cobalt waters glistened in the midday sun.

"You say this is an original Annex cottage?" Pruett asked.

"Yes; Mapleview is one of the '83 originals."

"And has the roof been replaced since '83?"

"No," Elliott acknowledged. "The kitchen was added in '89 and we repainted this summer, but no other renovations have been made to the original structure."

"Doesn't matter, really," Pruett remarked, his dark eyes resting upon the distant smoky blue shore of the Lower Peninsula. "I need a cottage; I've no time to build one, and yours is the only respectable cottage for sale at present. I'll offer you a fair price – more than fair. But you must tell me – how can you bear to sell it?"

"Because I must," Elliott shrugged. "No doubt you've endeavored to learn my situation?"

"I know of the bank failure."

"Then you know I sell from necessity, and that I will accept your fair offer unless I receive one better."

"I'll better it – whatever the offer," Pruett declared.

"Will you tell me why you must have a cottage this summer?" Elliott ventured.

"For my wife – I promised her. I shouldn't speak of such things—Prissy would be livid to hear me now—but as it's quite common knowledge in Indianapolis and I haven't had a decent conversation with another adult in over a month... You see, I hurt my wife egregiously. I became reckless and she was shamed when the affairs became public.

"Now you think me a bounder; I suppose I am. But I love my wife, Mr. Maier; I want her to be content. I'll give her this cottage – and she'll love it; we all will. My Emmeline will love that front bedroom; her brothers will make do with the smaller room until we can expand. We'll string a hammock between the southern porch railings, and maybe add a glider to watch the sunsets in comfort. In the cool evenings, we'll gather around the sitting room's fireplace telling stories or playing parlor games."

Elliott listened appreciatively, believing Pruett saw more in Mapleview's rooms than he had previously acknowledged.

"It was my most ardent hope that Mapleview would go to a family who would love it as we have," Elliott murmured.

"And we will – that is my most ardent hope. If my family is granted even a fraction of the fond memories you obviously have of the place, we shall be blessed. Shall we have our lawyers arrange terms, then?"

"I am an attorney, and will be happy to work with your lawyer. I hope you did not wish to claim the house this season, though? Iva and I intend to remain here for the summer."

"Of course," Pruett nodded. "We have rooms at the Grand through August and had not expected to claim ownership until summer's end."

"We've an understanding, then," Elliott offered Pruett his hand to shake. "Thank you for being so accommodating."

"Would you advise me on a few matters before I take my leave?" Pruett asked.

"Of course," Elliott leaned back against the smooth, cradling spindles of his rocking chair, his gaze returning to the water.

"What do you cottagers do for the entire summer?"

"What do we do?" Elliott frowned.

"You can't spend all hours escorting your wives to balls at Grand Hotel. What activities fill your days?"

"Some Annex neighbors are attempting to form a golf club. Many of them have yachts."

"Where do they sail these yachts?"

"They cruise around the Straits or down to Petoskey with the ladies."

"And without the ladies?"

Elliott sympathized with the hopeful tone of Pruett's question.

"Fishing around Les Cheneaux Islands, or further excursions. Next Tuesday Hugh Pendleton and I, with our elder sons, will embark upon a fishing trip to Lake Superior."

"The largest of the five Great Lakes," Pruett spoke with enthusiasm. "I'd like to see it some day."

"Why don't you join us?" Elliott spoke impulsively. "You and your sons?"

"Do you mean it?"

Pruett's face lost all dark and swarthy traces, his hopeful expression honest and genuine. Elliott found himself liking the man to whom he must relinquish his beloved cottage. No doubt his mother would disapprove of his association with the pompous philanderer, but Elliott thought Iva might like him – or at least own that Franklin Pruett was the best steward they could have hoped to find for Mapleview.

Del jogged down the broad stairs from bluff top to hotel lawn, but refrained from sprinting across the grass. Once he reached the cover of the small copse of woods, he hastened his step. They hadn't spoken of it or planned it, but both Del and Priscilla had been drawn back to that curve of southwestern shore every afternoon since their first encounter there.

Three o'clock on a sunny July day is the perfect time – Del had written the line in his notebook yesterday. He wanted to capture that sentiment in his novel—how the water shimmered under three o'clock's sun, its utter lack of obligation—an aimless hour drifting languidly between lunch and tea—and its subsequent freedom. No one looked for you at three o'clock; you weren't expected anywhere at that ambiguous hour. Three o'clock was an optimistic hour, a time when evening plans might not be settled, when any prospect was still possible. At three o'clock, a young man could meet a divinely beautiful married woman on the beach and forget every other hour of the day.

Del usually arrived first, but today Priscilla awaited him. She stood pensive and still as a statue gazing out to the horizon while the wind wreaked havoc with her skirts, made the lace and feathers of her hat dance wildly, and drew wisps of ash-blonde hair from her careful arrangement.

"What a glorious afternoon for thy fair Priscilla," he spoke reverently of the view they now shared.

"Yes, it's lovely," she murmured, turning to stroll north along the stone shore.

"Is something wrong?" Del immediately sensed her ill humor; Priscilla's current mood was one he had not yet encountered.

"Oh, no," he perceived her light tone as contrived, but did not object when she took his arm and drew closer to him. "Nothing of significance. A new family checked into the Grand this morning – I'm sure you'll see them soon. Such a handsome couple would be hard to miss. And their children! They held hands like little angels as they obediently followed their parents up the steps. Two girls and a little boy with the loveliest curly hair – and matching clothes! How on earth did she manage it? I've never been able to convince my children to don matching clothes, let alone hold hands! Franklin certainly noticed the woman's perfect hourglass figure; I encountered him this morning ogling her. He has no sense of propriety, no notion of discretion."

"And no appreciation for beauty if he could look upon any woman beside his wife."

"Dear, sweet boy," her hand upon his forearm constricted in affectionate squeeze.

"Why do you call me a boy? You cannot be more than five or six years older than me."

"You *are* a sweet boy!" Priscilla cried. "Not a day older than twenty-six."

"I'll be twenty-four in September – only six years from thirty."

"Yes, but I'll be thirty-seven at the end of August."

"Good gracious! If you're that old, of course I'm a boy! I should be addressing you as 'ma'am.' Ought I to have a chaperone?"

"You really should," she drawled, letting him draw her into a small grove of cedars for a soft, playful kiss.

Seven

Miss Verity Bennett of Bennettsville, Vermont let her gaze drift to the table Polly shared with Patsy Webb, Mrs. Vandermeer and Miss Vandermeer. How she longed to be with them! Verity's new friends—who met for bridge and euchre games on the porch—were geriatric. They could barely keep their drooping eyelids from closing in sleep; Mrs. Wannamaker yawned twice before dessert! Verity's friends met on the tennis courts were far livelier, but they were also married. They were an integral part of that unit—the married couple—and must therefore dine only with other couples.

Especially as they grew older, Verity appreciated Polly's energy. Polly was always game for adventure or activity. Of course, Polly was also partially to blame for Verity never having achieved coupledom of her own. Even though he died in the war like John Easton, she would at least have known what it felt like to be part of a couple were it not for Polly's predilection to claim every man as her beau. Widows were held in far greater esteem than spinsters, particularly outside of Bennettsville, Vermont. On Mackinac Island no one knew that her grandfather was the Revolutionary War hero who bequeathed his name to the lovely, little town she hailed from. She wasn't the most prosperous lady of the first family in town; here she was merely an old spinster. And judging by the nodding heads and half-closed eyes across the table, Verity knew she would be attending this Saturday's ball alone – and not one young man would feel obliged to ask her for a dance.

Polly stayed up for the ball. She sat between Patsy Webb and Mrs. Vandermeer, laughing and chatting as though nothing troubled her conscience. Verity settled upon a chair just inside the Casino doors with a prime view of the dance floor and of everyone's entrance and exit. Before long enough couples crowded the floor to block Polly's irksome presence from Verity's sight.

Didn't Miss Vandermeer look pleased as punch to be escorted into the casino by that striking, young sporting man? What a fine figure he possessed – tall, but not inconveniently so, and perfectly proportioned. His thick, chestnut hair, classical profile and intriguing hazel eyes drew many feminine glances. It goaded Verity to distraction that Polly knew his name and situation from Patsy Webb, when she had failed to discover any detail of the strapping, young man.

Mrs. Pruett certainly admired him. She had granted her debonair husband a rare dance, but her gaze followed the sporting man's progress throughout their waltz.

Miss Vandermeer led the young man (Miss Collins trailing in their wake) to the small assemblage centered around Miss Lillis Halloran. Introductions were made – with smiles and flushes and the thrill of meeting new potential dancing partners. The tallest, darkest, most handsome of the young men asked Miss Vandermeer for a dance. He took up her card and appeared to write his name next to multiple dances. She made a feeble swipe at his hands, but accepted the card he returned to her with shyly admiring smile.

The sporting man spread his name among the young ladies' dance cards. Verity admired his posture and athleticism as he twirled that strange Miss Collins around the floor to a lively polka.

A new couple contested Mrs. Adelia Alston's dominance of the dance floor tonight. He was handsome, but she was beautiful – with her crown of golden hair, her cheeks flushed with the joy of youth, her rose gown accentuating her enviable hourglass figure. Her radiant, upturned face smiled upon her husband, bestowing him with a reflection of her glory. Aside from a waltz with Mr. Jimmy Hayes, the charming little hotel manager, the blonde beauty danced only with her husband. Verity—who upon their arrival thought them quite common—now felt she would like to meet the attractive, young couple.

Verity tapped her foot restlessly, safe in the confidence that her skirt hid the instinctive movement. She was unaccustomed to sitting idly by watching others dance. The young men of Bennettsville felt obliged to ask a dance of their town founder's descendent. Everyone in Bennettsville knew Verity's fondness of dancing and lightness of foot. But no one on Mackinac Island—or anywhere else beyond Bennettsville county limits—knew of or cared about Miss Verity Bennett's penchant for dancing.

Admittedly, most of her interactions with the stiff, awkward youths and portly first citizens of Bennettsville could hardly be considering "dancing." Even had their steps been correct or possessed a trace of grace, they were nothing more than ceremonious. Devoid of emotion (save embarrassment from the young men!), Verity considered all post-war dances poor imitations. They blurred together as too insignificant for distinct recall. But Verity remembered each reel and waltz with Hezekiah Sanderson. She had thought of them so often they were burned into her conscious – a part of her. Her gaze drifted among the waltzing couples in Grand Hotel's casino ballroom, wondering, speculating... Were any of them creating such a memory tonight? Would any of them look back upon this ball with poignant longing, recognizing it as one of the finest hours of their youth?

Eight

It was most impertinent," Allyne declared, meeting Lou's jaded, gray eyes in the dressing table mirror as her maid strategically pinned her dark brown hair. "He had only met me the once – at that Feast Day of St. Anne Halloran affair. Yet he presumed to write himself in for all of my waltzes."

"The nerve of him!" Lou egged her on. "That Cassius Kearney."

"He actually asked me to call him 'Cass' as his friends do. What a smug, yet utterly common name."

"Is it?" Lou frowned. "I've never met a Cass or Cassius."

"Well I assure you, it is."

"I suppose it doesn't matter either way; you're not likely to suffer Mr. Kearney's company too often."

"Actually," Allyne averted her gaze from the uncomfortably perceptive gray eyes in the mirror. "He'll be part of our foursome on the Annex Links this afternoon."

"Will he?" Lou raised a provocative brow.

"I'm going for Lillis' sake," Allyne declared. "She's developed quite an admiration for Del and asked me to invite him to golf with Cass and her."

"Of course," Lou nodded solemnly, though she averted her gaze from the sharp mahogany eyes in the mirror. "It's so kind of you – to endure Mr. Kearney's presence for the sake of your new friend."

"Miss Halloran is the only society I have on Mackinac Island – aside from Del and Miss Collins."

Their eyes met once more in shared smirk.

"Actually, I'm rather fond of Lillis," Allyne acknowledged. "She's charming and fun. I've never had a friend who was truly fun. Something always held them back – some reservation, some well-concealed fear. Lillis has no fears and it's easy to forget yours in her presence. She'd take Fifth Avenue if she ever attempted its conquest."

"That's high praise, indeed," Lou nodded.

"That's a thought . . ." Allyne murmured, rising to tower over her petite maid. "I could invite Lillis to visit New York in October – return to town in triumph. Who would remember that Milton jilted me for Josie with Miss Lillis Halloran to distract them?"

"An excellent idea," Lou handed Allyne her hat as her mistress swept from the room.

Del waited in the vast porch's center, leaning against a pillar near the front steps, his eye on the open parlor doors. He caught sight of her tweed skirt flouncing down the staircase and straightened his broad shoulders. Allyne Vandermeer cut an elegant stride, even in her sporty golfing costume. Despite his perfect posture, Del only had two inches on Allyne, and he stood just a half inch under six feet.

"Good day," she nodded.

"Good day," he offered his arm, escorting her down the steps to the waiting victoria.

"You've played this course before?" Del asked, settling beside her on the smooth, leather seat.

"It's not much of a 'course' – just five links. It's quite pretty, though."

Allyne's words blended with the horse's hooves as their carriage cleared the portico. Del's eyes lifted to meet Priscilla's. She stood at the porch railing watching their approach. Del had told her of his plans for the afternoon; he had no secrets from Priscilla. She said Misses Vandermeer and Halloran made far better material for his novel and had encouraged him to accept their invitation for today's golf outing. Priscilla's tone had been so light, her countenance so unruffled, Del couldn't decide if she was jealous or not – until now, watching her austere gaze following their victoria as it rolled past.

"Del?"

"I'm sorry?" he turned toward Allyne, his expression composed.

"I asked if you were acquainted with Mrs. Pruett?"

"Who?" Del felt the flush creep into his cheeks despite his best repressive efforts.

"Mrs. Pruett – the beautiful blonde woman watching our carriage with such interest."

"Yes," Del recovered. "I'm acquainted with Mr. and Mrs. Pruett through my stepfather; they're from Indianapolis."

They lapsed into silence for a minute as the carriage climbed the gentle incline of West Bluff Road, each admiring their surroundings.

"What do you think of this little island?" Allyne asked in guardedly hopeful tone; she seemed embarrassed to acknowledge that she liked Mackinac Island, yet longed for him to validate her affection for the place.

"I think it's my favorite place in the world," Del declared, realizing that he meant it.

"The air is as fresh as the Alps, but with that sweet lake scent," Allyne impressed him with her perceptions. "I feel as though we're on the frontier – I imagine bands of hostile Indians prowling the shores of that Upper Peninsula. And yet we golf among these sacred woods and dance under the island's stars."

"What a line!" Del favored Allyne with fond, appreciative smile. "May I use it in my novel?"

"You tease me."

"No – it was a beautifully expressed sentiment."

"You're welcome to it," she shrugged.

Allyne lifted her right arm to wave to a lady on the veranda they ambled past. Del thought it the island's finest cottage, with its fish scale shingling, its covered balconies, tower and bays.

"That's Pine Bluff," Allyne informed him. "That was Lillis' aunt, Adelia Alston. I had the honor of attending her recent kettledrum."

"I've seen her at the Saturday balls," Del recalled.

"Miss Collins thinks Lillis the island princess, but it's really Adelia Alston."

"Is she so presumptuous?"

"Oh, no! She's actually quite captivating. The greatest

beauty I've ever beheld. A mother of three children, but she seems as fun as Lillis."

"Lillis," Del vaguely remembered being introduced to the young blonde at Saturday's ball; he had danced with her once, but it must have been one of the livelier numbers that discouraged conversation. "You consider her fun?"

"You'll see," Allyne assured him with maddeningly vague grin.

Del saw, fifteen minutes later as he and Allyne greeted Lillis Halloran and Cass Kearney. Lillis wasn't stunningly beautiful like Priscilla Pruett, but her face made him look twice – smooth, ivory skin, jade green eyes enhanced by thick, dark lashes and hair as golden as an October meadow. Yet these physical attributes would be common without the lively spirit animating their present curves and lines.

"Miss Halloran," Del bowed. "Mr. Kearney," he shook the taller man's hand.

"No one is a 'Miss' or 'Mr.' on the links," Lillis proclaimed. "Today we are Lillis and Cass, Allyne and Del."

They murmured greetings as they met the young caddies upon the first tee. After their fourth drives, Del suspected that Lillis hit her balls in the direction of his deliberately. Intrigued, he strolled beside her to the edge of the east woods. He had never been pursued in such obvious manner, and yet he felt flattered rather than annoyed.

"You love the island," Del observed, falling into step beside Lillis as they approached the fifth tee.

"All of my best memories are here," Lillis spoke candidly. "My grandparents built Lakeview when I was three. To me, Mackinac Island is synonymous with summer. I've always felt this island was special. The local Indians think it a sacred place. I feel greater capacity for joy exists on this island – great capacity for love and hope."

Her genuine emotion made Lillis' words more poignant and powerful. Her affection for this island emanated from her fresh, young face, from her bright eyes and lithe, brisk step. Del made the connection involuntarily, and knew from this day forward he would see Lillis Halloran's twinkling, jade eyes and rose-lipped smirk when he thought of Mackinac Island.

"Allyne tells me you're writing a novel?" Lillis inquired as they strolled down the Annex road – after she had ceased her triumphant whoops and victorious cheers for winning her bets. Both Cass and Allyne had to ante up $5 after Lillis' score was five strokes lower than Allyne's.

"Yes," Del nodded.

"Is it any good?"

Del thought her audacious until he glanced over and saw her mischievous grin; he had learned from the links today that Lillis enjoyed taunting and teasing.

"It's a masterpiece," he returned. "Better than Twain."

"Is it set on Mackinac Island?"

"Where else could it be set?"

"Then I suppose we're in it," Lillis sighed.

"What gives you such a supposition?"

"You said it was a masterpiece."

He laughed; he couldn't contain the outburst. Allyne was right – Lillis was fun.

"Though if I'm honest, I can't imagine a novel about

Mackinac Island without at least one or two Hallorans making an appearance," Lillis resumed. "Unless it's to be set in the past? Perhaps it involves voyageurs or red-coated British soldiers?"

"It's contemporary," Del informed her – he thought it would be, when he started writing it.

"Well, then – it's bound to be inspired by Hallorans. Will you give us a nicer name, though?"

"O'Halloran?" he offered.

"Heavens! You wouldn't!"

"I rather like the sound of it."

"That was our name," Lillis informed him. "Back in Ireland. Grandpa told us he lost the 'O' at sea. I always imagined it as a big, white life preserver, bobbing over the Atlantic waves, growing smaller and smaller as the ship steamed away. I used to feel sad for that poor lost 'O', but Halloran is bad enough on its own."

"I'm sure I'll think of another name in time," Del offered as they ambled up the front walk to Sunset Cottage.

"I'm not sure that you've observed enough Hallorans," Lillis declared. "You ought to attend Grandpa's seventieth birthday party – it's the Tuesday after next. There will be dancing and a fireworks show and all the Hallorans congregated together. Just mind how much punch you drink if you want to make it to the fireworks show."

"I wouldn't miss it."

They paused at the foot of the porch steps, their eyes meeting briefly before turning to look up the path. Allyne and Cass—engaged in conversation—had fallen twenty yards behind Del and Lillis' brisk pace. Allyne's smile and flushed cheeks indicated susceptibility to Kearney's charm – or whatever it was. Del admired Cass Kearney's confidence and energy, but charming was the last word he connected with the earnestly ambitious businessman. And yet the sophisticated Fifth Avenue creation flushed like a farmer's daughter in his most singular attention.

"She told me she thought Cass most 'impertinent,'" Lillis laughed as Allyne and Cass loitered up the front walk. "But she doesn't seem to mind his impertinence today, does she?"

Miss Verity Bennett pounced upon Miss Collins, interrupting the young lady's committed vigil at the porch railing. Undaunted by Miss Collins's dark expression, Verity presented a broad, inviting smile. No doubt the young lady would rather spend the afternoon brooding, but Verity had other uses for her.

"Miss Collins? It's Miss Bennett – we met on the archeological tour."

"Good afternoon," the girl managed.

"I was hoping you could assist me? I'm in dire need of a euchre partner. Do you know the game?"

"Yes," Miss Collins nodded.

"But are you any good? I like to win, you see."

"As do I."

Bertha took a second look at Miss Bennett. She had dismissed her as a fat, old spinster, but now decided her thick, silver hair and large, mahogany eyes gave her an air of distinction, even elegance. And wasn't she from the east? Was she acquainted with Miss Vandermeer? With a last westward glance, Bertha reluctantly agreed to be Miss Bennett's euchre partner.

"I knew when I first saw you that you were a lady who liked to win," Verity flattered the girl as they strolled down the long porch toward the card tables. "A raven-haired lass will always win, especially against blondes. Let us challenge these two...

"Mrs. Pruett, isn't it? It's Miss Bennett. We met on the archeological tour, though I feel better acquainted with Mr. Pruett and your charming sons after sharing their carriage that afternoon. It seems you and your lovely acquaintance are in need of opponents?"

"Yes," Priscilla Pruett returned the older woman's amiable smile. "Please join us? And may I present my new friend, Mrs. Rose Harris, of Chicago?"

"Pleased to meet you," Mrs. Harris rose from her chair to bow in greeting; Verity appreciated when the young showed proper respect and favored the beautiful blonde with fond smile.

"And may I present my new friend, Miss Bertha Collins of . . ."

"Peoria," the girl replied, taking the chair across from Verity's after her elders had seated themselves.

"Forgive my insolence," Verity's eager tone negated her request. "I ask only out of concern for their health – where are your handsome sons and their father? I noticed you dined without them last night."

"On a fishing excursion in the Upper Peninsula," Mrs. Pruett could not quite keep the smile from her expression as she handed Verity the thin deck of cards. "They'll be gone a week."

"Won't you miss them?" Mrs. Harris asked. "I can't imagine being away from my children for a whole week!"

"They must be quite young," Priscilla remarked, taking the deck back from Verity when dealt the first Jack.

"Cecilia is nine, Juliet seven and Arthur only five," Mrs. Harris replied.

"Your girls should meet my Emmeline – she's eight and would be thrilled to show them around the hotel. And Francis is six; he and Arthur could be chums," Mrs. Pruett declared.

"Shall we bring them together tomorrow afternoon?" Mrs. Harris asked hopefully, sweeping a trick from the table and adding it to her stack.

"I have other plans tomorrow afternoon," Mrs. Pruett trumped Verity's ace of spades. "But let's meet in the morning? Say . . . half past ten? On the lawn?"

"We'll be there," Rose Harris spoke as she adjusted the scorecards to give the blondes two more points.

Verity decided to reevaluate her theory on raven-haired lasses winning, for Miss Collins—even when graced with good cards—was in too distracted a mental state to play them strategically.

"You're missing your friend this afternoon," Verity remarked, by now wholly unsympathetic to the girl who had dealt her three nines. "Miss Vandermeer stepped out earlier today with Mr. – I can't recall his name, Mr. . . . "

"Drury," Priscilla Pruett's prompt response drew curious glances from her companions at the card table. "Del Drury; I'm acquainted with his mother and stepfather in Indianapolis."

"Yes, Mr. Drury," Verity nodded as she shuffled the cards (admiring Bertha afresh for sliding the cards to her across the table when it should have been Mrs. Pruett's deal). "They looked en route to some sporting endeavor."

"They went golfing with Lillis Halloran and Cass Kearney," Bertha's bitter tone had no correlation to the cards in her hand; she told Verity to pick up the Nine of Spades and announced her intention of taking on their opponents alone for the potential four points.

"Halloran?" Mrs. Harris's radiant, young face brightened. "Is she related to Mr. Brennan Halloran?"

"Her uncle," Miss Collins informed them as she scooped in the tricks.

"My husband befriended Brennan at Northwestern and they were business associates for a time after," Mrs. Harris announced, her jaw tilted slightly up in her pride of the connection.

"Did you attend their Feast Day of St. Anne celebration last week?" Miss Collins asked, putting the lady with small claim to the Hallorans in her place as she won her fifth trick.

"We've only been here a week," Mrs. Harris shrugged off the question and the four points Verity gleefully added to her scorecards. "We haven't seen Mr. Halloran yet. Of course we would like to, but our primary focus this summer is our children. Back home Harland's work occupies so much of his time and I'm plagued with social obligations; Harland and I have determined to devote our time on Mackinac to our dear children."

Verity perceived Priscilla Pruett's affront to these lofty words and commiserated with her sentiment. Mrs. Harris exuded an aura of perfection that seemed unlikely to manifest in reality. She and her husband were certainly young and beautiful, and their children were more doll than human in their exemplary appearance and behavior, but Verity sensed the woman's vulnerability beneath her smooth veneer. Rose Harris seemed to be trying just a bit too hard to leave the impression that her life lived up to her name.

"You didn't wish to accompany your friend Miss Vandermeer?" Mrs. Pruett asked Miss Collins, with subtle crack in her casual tone.

"I don't golf," Miss Collins shrugged, shuffling the cards with distracted vehemence. "Of course she would have invited me if I golfed. Lillis and I have been friends for years; she only met Miss Vandermeer this summer. Though today's outing is more of a matchmaking endeavor. Lillis fancies Mr. Drury, who is acquainted with Miss Vandermeer from his time in New York, and her friend Anne's brother admires Miss Vandermeer. Were they engaged in any other endeavor, of course Lillis would have included me. But—as I said—I don't golf."

"Are you traveling with family, as well, Miss Bennett?" Mrs. Harris asked in overly cheerful note to counter Bertha's intense, snappish tone.

"I have no family," Verity's response wiped that mask of a smile off the young woman's face.

"None at all?" Miss Collins blurted without thought – so like Polly that it irked Verity beyond the impropriety of both question and protocol; well-mannered young ladies did not ask such impudent questions of their elders.

"Both of my brothers were killed at Gettysburg before marrying, my beau fell at the Second Battle of Bull Run, and my parents died years ago," Verity informed them; at least Bertha had the grace to flush with shame.

"I'm so very sorry for your losses," Mrs. Pruett offered, genuine compassion emanating from her pretty blue eyes. "Our nation owes your brave brothers and beau a debt of gratitude for their service and sacrifice."

"Thank you," Verity blinked back looming tears. "The Bennetts have always devoted ourselves to the American cause. My grandfather served with distinction under General Washington; the town of Bennettsville changed its name to honor its most acclaimed Patriot."

"How sad," Mrs. Harris couldn't blink her tears dry, though they did not spill over her lids. "The man who fought for our nation's Independence lost both of his grandsons in that nation's Civil War."

"It's sad for my family, but I prefer to think of the thousands of souls set free by my brothers' sacrifice. They didn't have heirs, but look at the legacy left to their country. Not to mention the town of Bennettsville."

"You honor them well," Mrs. Pruett observed.

"Are you traveling on your own, then?" Mrs. Harris pried.

"I might as well be," Verity grumbled, all sympathetic notions for Mrs. Pruett evaporating as the woman trumped her ace of hearts for the euchre.

"I thought you were traveling with Mrs. Easton?" Mrs. Pruett murmured to Verity's further chagrin.

"In that we are sharing a suite of rooms for the summer – yes, but I have not spoken a word to her since our arrival on Mackinac."

"But you've been here over a month," Bertha's latest blurt nearly caused Verity to lose her temper. "You've been sharing a suite for over a month and haven't said one word to each other?"

"She may have spoken to me," Verity shrugged as she shuffled the cards. "But I can assure you I never responded."

"You were the injured party in your quarrel?" Mrs. Pruett's empathetic tone placated Verity.

"I was," she nodded solemnly.

"And you can't forgive her?" Mrs. Harris's question seemed condescending to Verity – what did little Miss Perfect know of heartbreak and betrayal?

"She's never asked for it," Verity snapped. "Of course Christian charity would compel me to forgive her if she asked to be forgiven."

"Does she know this? Forgive me," Mrs. Pruett earnestly entreated. "I ask because I should like to discuss the matter with her. Perhaps if she knew an appeal for forgiveness would end your quarrel—"

"She does know it, but doesn't believe her actions require forgiveness. But by all means, discuss the matter with her," Verity shrugged.

"They're back," Miss Collins announced, rising to her feet to better observe Allyne Vandermeer and Del Drury alighting from the carriage.

"And what does that matter?" Verity snapped. "We're one point away from winning this game, so sit right back down and pick up your cards, if you please."

Miss Collins looked mutinous, but obeyed the older woman long enough to lose the game on a renege. Verity watched the girl run up the porch to intercept Miss Vandermeer and Mr. Drury through narrowed eyes. Her inclination toward Bertha Collins had hitherto been neutral; Verity now actively disliked her.

Del Drury chose a rocking chair at the shaded east end of the world's longest front porch and broke the seal of his mother's much anticipated response. Her letter was filled with the usual cautions – was it wise to quit his job so hastily? And spend all of his publishing proceeds on an expensive hotel for the entire summer? She also offered to speak to her husband about a job in his store.

You can earn a good living by day and write in the evenings, Amaryllis wrote in scrawl possessing just enough refinement to be considered elegant script rather than sloppy scratching; Del scowled as he deciphered. His mother's creativity only extended to home and wardrobe; she had no concept of writing as an art form, nor the pains (and pleasures) endured in creation of a single page. He skipped over her good-natured (if futile) advice until finding the paragraph he sought:

You asked if I knew the source of the Pruetts' animosity. I do not like to spread gossip, but as everyone in town knows of the incident, I see no harm in answering your inquiry. And naturally I've heard everything, for the confrontation occurred just outside my husband's store! I've since learned Franklin Pruett's philandering was common knowledge among the town's gentlemen, but until his two mistresses' physical altercation just outside Holderson's Dry Goods Emporium, the town matrons had been blissfully ignorant. The widow, Mrs. Ethel Walker, attacked Mrs. Amos King. The unfortunate scene took place just two days after the Pruetts' fifteenth wedding anniversary ball, which both Mr. and Mrs. King attended. My sympathies are entirely with poor Priscilla. Women with her beauty often inspire envy and I'm afraid most of her friends and acquaintances spitefully reveled in the blow to Mrs. Pruett's pride – she did have such an abundance of it.

Yes, she did – Del agreed with his mother's observation. His flattery and affection must appeal to Priscilla's pride, but that same pride held him at arm's length. Was she too averse to committing her husband's sin to avenge it? Or would she sacrifice her self-righteous virtue for what her heart desired?

"Del?" Allyne Vandermeer greeted him, sinking gracefully upon the rocker next to his as he hastily tucked the folded letter into his breast pocket.

"Allyne, I trust you—"

"Never mind any of that now. I've managed to elude Bertha for the moment, but she'll no doubt join us soon."

"She obviously annoys you – why do you endure her? Why not cut her? You could easily manage it."

"I couldn't," Allyne shook her head, her heavy lids guarding what might have been a sensitive expression. "I thought I should, but I'd never treat someone like… at any rate, I feel obliged to be kind. Which is why I wanted to extend the invitation out of her presence."

"Invitation?"

"Kitty and Rob Kearney have invited us to join their yachting party tomorrow."

"Kitty and Rob invited us?"

"As guests of Lillis and Cass. Oh, Lord – here she comes . . ." Allyne rose to her feet, facing Bertha Collins' approaching figure. "We're to rendezvous at Lakeview Cottage at ten o'clock. Meet me by the porch steps at quarter of if you'd like to ride over with me."

Del watched Allyne's tall, elegant figure glide up the porch to graciously greet Miss Collins. His relief expanded when the ladies turned to stroll in the opposite direction. He followed them as far as the porch steps, which Del descended, waited for a carriage to pass, and jogged across the road and down the bluff-side steps.

Priscilla awaited him on the beach. Her sky blue eyes brightened as a smile alighted upon her beautiful face. Most of Priscilla's smiles were a little sly, with the allure of a siren, but this one possessed an angelic quality. Moved by her expression, Del lifted her hand to his lips in age-old gesture of courtly love.

"You're in a very fine mood today," she observed.

"I was about to express the same observation of you – your smile was radiant just now."

"Of course it was," Priscilla took his extended arm to stroll up the beach. "I saw you."

Del's heart swelled in his chest, though he knew she only meant to flirt with him.

"I must attribute my improved spirits to my husband's absence. He left for the U.P. with Monty and Gil yesterday; they'll be gone a week."

This time Del's heart stopped for the few seconds their eyes met in shared glance.

"And I've had a rather amusing—or at least interesting—afternoon."

"How so?" Del asked.

"I played euchre with Miss Verity Bennett, Miss Bertha Collins, and the relatively new entity of Rose Harris."

"She's an entity, is she?"

"Oh, yes," Priscilla nodded emphatically. "She's a blast of youth and beauty, so sweet and kind. With the perfect husband, the perfect children, the perfect life. And she condescends to us weaker mortals – appalled that we are glad of a week's reprieve from our husband or not on speaking terms with our travel companion.

"Of course I envy her – she has the life I always wanted. But as I waited for you today it occurred to me that all her perfection might not be genuine. I realized that my view of the Harris family was the image of the Pruett family I strove to project back in Indianapolis. Perhaps Mrs. Harris's illusion is as flimsy as mine, though there is no denying how uncannily well-behaved her children are."

"Who isn't on speaking terms with their travel companion?" Del inquired.

"Miss Bennett, of Bennettsville, Vermont. She's also quite a charismatic entity. A proud woman who cannot bear any blight upon her honor – not even to lose a euchre match! You should have seen the daggers she glared at her inept, young partner. Yet I found her otherwise charming. She's much friendlier than Mrs. Easton, though I can't forget the latter's words from our first meeting during the archeological tour – whatever their quarrel, Mrs. Easton thinks it inconsequential, but knows it means a great deal to Miss Bennett. I hope to learn what they quarreled about at some point this summer, but it's odd not speaking to your lifelong friend and travel companion for nearly a month.

"Speaking of odd… Miss Collins."

"What about Miss Collins?" Del asked.

"You're acquainted with her, are you not? Don't you find her odd? She's so…intense. I found her disconcerting. And her preoccupation with Miss Lillis Halloran is strange."

"It's more than preoccupation," Del remarked. "I'd say we've reached the level of obsession."

"Is Miss Halloran so fascinating?" Priscilla asked, her tone dismissive, though Del knew she listened attentively for his response.

"She's an entity," Del returned. "And, to Miss Collins, the paragon of ladies. Lillis is prettier than Bertha, has more friends than Bertha, more money, finer clothes, better manners and many other talents lost to Bertha. Miss Halloran's superiority is exacerbated on this island, where her family occupies four of its finest cottages and dominates the social scene."

"She fancies you," Priscilla declared, her hand sliding down his arm to entwine her fingers with his.

"Miss Collins?" he laughed.

"Lillis."

"She's a little flirt, but Lillis doesn't fancy me," Del scoffed.

"She does," Priscilla maintained. "Miss Collins told us so explicitly over our euchre game."

"And you believe Miss Collins' perception regarding Lillis Halloran's interaction with anyone?" Del chided.

"Fair point," Priscilla conceded as he drew her through a gap in the cedars to kiss her.

"You're the most beautiful woman I've ever beheld," Del declared, fitting his hands around her heart-shaped face. "Do you know what your kisses mean to me?"

"Yes," her smile suddenly showed each of her thirty-six years.

"Priscilla..."

"We should return," she pulled one of his hands from her cheek to guide him back along the stone-strewn shore.

"Perhaps tomorrow, we could meet earlier?" Priscilla ventured. "I could have a picnic basket packed."

"I can't see you tomorrow," Del confessed. "I've been invited on a Halloran yachting excursion, and I've agreed to escort Miss Vandermeer."

"How exciting," Priscilla's tone was perfectly light, as though it mattered little to her when or if she saw him again. "And such a fine prospect for literary inspiration."

"The only reason I'm going," Del replied in tone he hoped as equally light.

"Of course the fair Lillis Halloran will be in attendance."

Del strove to mask all outward signs of elation – she was jealous! Mrs. Priscilla Pruett was jealous of the time he spent in Miss Halloran's company!

"Of course," he drawled. "No doubt I have her to thank for my invitation – if she fancies me as Miss Collins claims."

"I thought we had agreed that Miss Collins' judgment cannot be trusted?" Priscilla wouldn't rise to his baiting tone.

"I'll see you in the ballroom?" Del asked at the woods' edge.

"Not tonight," Priscilla shook her head as she pinned her hat over her silken, blonde hair.

"Tomorrow, then? At the Saturday ball?" Del caught her hand before she could escape from the trees onto the hotel's vast lawn.

"No, I've another engagement."

"Sunday, then? On the beach?"

"Perhaps," she murmured evasively, pulling her hand free and stepping through the trees.

Del watched her march up the lawn, her white skirts swaying, her head held high. Priscilla hadn't mentioned any other island acquaintances; she couldn't have engagements tonight *and* tomorrow. She would have mentioned them – before he told her of his yachting excursion. Was she truly jealous? Or merely annoyed by the inconvenience? Del had no delusions that Priscilla loved him, but knew that she enjoyed his attentions. He was uncertain of the depth of her affection, but suspected it was inspired at least in part by vengeance for the husband who so recently humiliated her. Perhaps he might discover it Sunday; he would be waiting for her on their beach at three o'clock.

Nine

Franklin Pruett let the dancing flames mesmerize his gaze. Their low crackle as they devoured the logs drowned out Elliott Maier and Hugh Pendleton's banter from across the campfire. Franklin was immersed in the pine-scented wilderness. The sky above was darker and more star-filled than any he had beheld in recent memory. In the crisp, smoky air and warm glow of the campfire, he was conscious of nothing but his own thoughts.

Priscilla had been happy to see him go. Of course she was still angry with him, but Franklin perceived that more than a week's freedom from his presence inspired her smile when she waved their ferry off last Thursday. Though no more inclined to be amicable with her husband, Priscilla's looks and spirits had shown marked improvement over the last two weeks. She always dressed well and her beauty seemed everlasting, but lately it possessed a warmer quality, as though touched by some deep emotion.

Franklin had noticed how that good-looking sportsman admired his wife. He had thought Priscilla charitably indulging the young man when she danced with him at last Saturday's ball. But after observing Priscilla whenever this man was in their vicinity since the ball, Franklin concluded the admiration was mutual – and he was mad with jealousy. He didn't blame Priscilla for wanting retribution, but he longed to throttle that pompous, young sportsman. He had almost backed out of this fishing excursion, but Monty and Gil were too excited for the adventure by the time he felt any misgivings. The thought of Priscilla—his wife—in another man's arms made Franklin tremble with impotent fury.

Priscilla had tormented Franklin since their first meeting – first with her beauty, later with criticisms. Her cruelest act was to deny him her love after being so generous with it for so many years. He would not yearn for her smiles if he had never basked in them; he would not miss her sweet lips if he had not kissed them so often. And now she kissed that damned sportsman and he was stuck up here in the middle of nowhere.

A hearty chuckle from across the crackling campfire distracted Franklin from his torrid thoughts; Elliott and Hugh laughed over another shared memory. They hadn't stopped reminiscing since embarking on this confounded venture. On the ferry to St. Ignace and the train to Sault Ste. Marie, the old Annex friends had recalled past visits to the Upper Peninsula—the "U.P."—with their fathers. Elliott and Hugh hoped their sons would be as impressed by the Soo Locks as they had been at that age. As it transpired, the engineering marvels of the locks were lost on their younger sons, though Hugh's nine-year-old son had showed as much interest as Monty and Gil. Sault Ste. Marie had been the last night Franklin slept under a roof. The following morning, they chartered a boat to take them across the bay to a small town called Paradise, from which they hiked to this spot in the north woods. Franklin envied Elliott and Hugh their memories and easy camaraderie. He had many acquaintances and associates, but no friends. Priscilla had been his only friend, but they hadn't been friendly in months.

"Forgive us, Franklin," Elliott called across the campfire. "You're no doubt weary of our old stories."

"You're fortunate to share so many fond recollections," Franklin offered.

"I thought our sons would have the same fond memories," Elliott's voice was husky with his sudden emotion.

"Just because they won't be at Mapleview doesn't mean we can't take them to the U.P. every summer," Hugh spoke bracingly.

"And aren't they forming their first fond recollection right now?" Franklin spoke to cheer the man whose beloved cottage he was to buy; damn the man for making him feel such guilt. "And your family will always be welcome at Mapleview."

"Thank you," Elliott nodded before lifting his gaze heavenward, perhaps to prevent any rogue tears from escaping his lids.

"Look!" he cried, his tone suddenly exuberant. "The Northern Lights!"

Franklin had never seen anything so awe-inspiring; he was as mesmerized by the green and gold rays of light pulsing in the patch of sky visible above the small clearing as he had been by the campfire a few minutes before.

"We'll have a better view of them at the lakeshore," Hugh declared, springing to his feet. "Should we wake Dad and the boys?"

"Yes," Franklin answered for Elliott, hastening to his tent to shake Monty and Gil from their heavy slumber.

Fathers and sons hastened down the path to the small beach, their faces upturned to the celestial dance in the north sky. The lights seemed to form patterns, like a kaleidoscope – ephemeral brushstrokes their Creator painted across the heavens. The extraordinary sight put things in perspective.

Franklin forgot his former grievances in the wonder of these Northern Lights. It didn't matter what Priscilla did with the sportsman – all that mattered was that he win her back. He had won her love once; he could do it again. And if he couldn't—if he was destined to be estranged from her—it was all worth it. They had Monty, Gil, Emmeline and Francis; their children were all that really mattered. Raising them to be good citizens, creating memories that they would fondly reminisce over in twenty years – in these endeavors Priscilla would never leave his side.

Northern Splendor impressed Allyne Vandermeer; Joseph Halloran's yacht was not as large as those her New York acquaintances sailed around Cannes and Monte Carlo, but she found its interior no less luxuriant. On its covered top deck, they sat upon bamboo chairs amidst potted ferns sipping glasses of lemonade that Allyne suspected to be laced with Halloran Whiskey. Or was it merely the abundant sunshine and sapphire waters that made her so giddy?

Though quite aware of Cass's dark eyes upon her, Allyne let the other passengers distract her. Aside from Allyne and Del, all other guests were either relations or old island friends. Allyne found herself envying their camaraderie. These Midwesterners had summered together at the same resort town since childhood just like her Newport acquaintances, yet they were friendly rather than competitive. They all genuinely seemed to like each other and reminisced over past summers with equal equanimity.

Lillis' sister, Kitty Kearney, commanded the crowd. Allyne found her lively and charming, but thought Lillis sold herself short in comparison. Lillis had declared Kitty the prettier, more charismatic sister; she claimed to live in Kitty's shadow, but Allyne thought Lillis far outshined the older, more refined sister.

"Would you walk with me?" Cass Kearney loomed above her chair, blocking her view of Kitty and Lillis.

Color rose to Allyne's cheeks, for she sensed the scrutiny from her fellow passengers. The sudden lull in conversation recommenced when she took Cass's arm to stroll from pavilion to open deck at the yacht's aft. Why must he make her conspicuous? He could have taken the ottoman beside her chair and conversed in relative privacy; instead he drew every eye to them – as if staking a public claim to her. And yet her cheeks flushed with pleasure to see Lily King's wistfully envious eyes follow their progress.

"How do you like our lakes, Allyne?" Cass asked in tone confident of her answer.

"There is something special about this pristine north country," Allyne replied, pausing beside him at the starboard railing and gazing out to the stark horizon line.

"Are you staying through the summer?" he inquired.

"Yes, through the first week of September. And you? Anne says you usually only spend a fortnight on the island."

"You've asked her about me, have you?"

Allyne railed against his teasing – as if she was the type of lady to ask about a businessman!

"Never, but your sister does have a regrettable habit of sharing more information than her listeners are entitled to or desirous of hearing. But I did just ask you a direct question, which you've thus far failed to answer."

"Well, then – that's me told off. I suppose I'll be staying through the first week of September."

"But—" Allyne bit her lower lip over the impulsive question.

"I haven't taken more than a two-week holiday since I started work at Kearney Packing," Cass informed her, presumably to impart the significance of his holiday plans this summer.

"That doesn't sound like much of a life," Allyne declared.

"Suits me just fine."

"Working at a meat packing company?" Allyne couldn't remove the disdain from her tone.

"A company my father built from the ground up! He came to this country with ten cents to his name."

"Yes, and of course you're proud of him, but he's enabled you to live a more enlightened life."

"How so?" Cass turned to meet her eyes.

"You've the means to travel – to see the wonders of the world. To experience the Paris opera and Russian ballet, see the ruins of Athens and Rome, the snow-capped peaks surrounding Alpine valleys. Don't you aspire to more?"

"Of course I do," Cass bristled.

"Then you agree? You'd be better removed from the business?"

"Removed? No. I'll assume responsibility for Kearney Packing when Father retires, but I'm not content to own a meat packing firm."

"Then perhaps we do agree?" Allyne asked hopefully.

"I plan to own the largest, most profitable meat packing firm in Chicago and all of the United States."

"But how can you advance in life tied to a meat packing company?" Allyne cried.

"Such eastern airs," Cass chided. "I believe your father works for his fortune?"

"Yes – and I can assure you his quality of life is quite low."

"If he likes his business, that is not its cause."

"How can it not be? When he would rather be on Wall Street than any street with his family?" Allyne blinked back looming tears.

"Do you resemble your father?" Cass's sudden change of topic perplexed Allyne, but sufficiently distracted her from her tears.

"No, they say I look very much like my mother."

"Perhaps your face is a constant reminder of his loss."

"I'm well aware of my father's aversion to my face."

"I only meant that instead of letting your face be a comfort to him, he allows it to remind him of the pain of your mother's death rather than the beauty of her life."

"How do you know her life had beauty?"

"If she looked like you, I know it did."

Allyne thought of her conversation with Cass on the Halloran yacht as she dressed for the Saturday ball and all through the church service the next morning. For a meat packer, Cass Kearney could express a fine sentiment. She had never thought of this theory—always ready to accept the blame—but now that Cass said it, it seemed obvious. Her father felt things deeply; Allyne was like him in that respect. She had come upon him with tear-filled eyes several times, and Grandmother Vandermeer had often accused her of being "as sensitive as your father at that age." Allyne had been so focused on how her father's neglect hurt her feelings that she had never bothered to consider his. It was certainly more romantic to think of him as a brokenhearted man still pining for his beloved—twenty-three years after her death—than to believe that he found her unloveable through some fault of her own.

When not thinking of their conversation on the yacht, Allyne recalled some of Cass's compliments. He never said anything conventional, which led to a perception of authenticity. Waltzing together Saturday, he told her she turned with such grace and seemed to float in his arms – that was one of her favorites. Allyne was as tall or taller than most of her dancing partners, but she had felt petite in Cass's sturdy arms; he really was the perfect height.

"Allyne!"

She spun around at Mrs. Vandermeer's outraged greeting. "Are you waiting for someone?"

Allyne stood at the top of the porch steps, her gaze fixed upon the road in obvious anticipation, with such focus that she had not even noticed her grandmothers alight from a carriage and climb the porch steps.

"Whom are you waiting for? Your friend, Lillis?" Mrs. Webb asked hopefully.

"Cass is taking me on a driving tour of the island sights," Allyne announced.

"Surely by now you've seen all the sights of this little island?" Mrs. Webb scoffed.

"And surely my granddaughter does not wait like a dog at the door for its master's return?" Mrs. Vandermeer managed to inflict as much flame as ice in her menacing tone.

"What are the rules of etiquette when awaiting a gentleman at a hotel where your room is half the length of the world's longest front porch?" Allyne's flippant response made her grandmother's nostrils flare.

"Certainly not this!" Mrs. Vandermeer struggled to keep her voice at respectable volume. "And why are you going driving with that swarthy Irish Papist?"

"Really, dear," Mrs. Webb spoke in more measured tone. "His Catholicism should rule him out as a suitor, even if he weren't an Irishman. Remember Bridget?"

Of course Allyne remembered Bridget. Her first maid had to be sacked after falling pregnant. Bridget had hoped to keep her employment by explaining that her lover (the chauffeur) planned to marry her, but Grandmother Vandermeer had shown no mercy – she would not have a woman with such loose morals around her granddaughter. Both Bridget and the chauffeur had been sacked and Allyne—annoyed to have a new maid to train two weeks before her debut—had vowed never to have another Irish maid.

"What on earth does Bridget have to do with anything?" Allyne bristled. "Yes, Cass is Irish and Catholic – which should be sufficient for you to realize nothing will come of this harmless courtship."

"But to be seen with him?" Mrs. Vandermeer persisted. "Does he smell of organs and entrails and dead flesh? Or has the clean northern air masked the factory's stench?"

"It's only a fancy," Allyne snapped. "I need some sort of entertainment on this little island. Here's his carriage – if you'll excuse me?"

Bertha Collins watched Allyne Vandermeer flounce down the porch steps in an angry huff that seemed to float away as Cassius Kearney helped her into the buggy. Lurking behind the portico pillar, Bertha had heard every word of Allyne's exchange with her grandmothers. A triumphant glow lit her round cheeks as Bertha watched their carriage drive off.

Should Allyne become too meddlesome, Bertha would threaten to tell Mr. Kearney how much his religion, Irish blood and factory stench bothered Miss Vandermeer – how he was "only a fancy" for her to pass the time this summer.

Bertha didn't believe these factors troubled Allyne as much as her grandmothers, but she was quite confident Allyne would not wish Mr. Kearney to hear of them. Or Lillis, for that matter! Lillis was also Irish Catholic – how warm would she feel toward Allyne if she knew of the easterner's disdain for her faith and heritage? And was there much distinction in Allyne's opinion between the stench of the Kearney meat factory and the Halloran distilleries?

Distracted by the appearance of Del Drury, Bertha subdued her elated thoughts and stepped around the pillar to greet him. How handsome he looked this afternoon in navy blazer that fitted his broad shoulders so well. A gust of wind lifted the straw boater from his thick, chestnut hair and Bertha was quick to scoop up the rogue hat from the porch floor. When Del's hazel eyes met hers, Bertha's heart skipped a beat.

"Miss Collins," his smile dazzled her as Bertha returned his hat. "Thank you."

"You're most welcome, Mr. Drury."

"It's Del," his smile faltered as his gaze drifted longingly toward the porch steps. "Thank you again."

"Are you going for a walk, Del?"

"Yes."

"I was just on my way to walk through the woods – may I join you?"

"It's more of a hike I had in mind," Del demurred. "Far too strenuous of a pace for a lady. Another time, perhaps?"

And with a lift of the straw boater, Del jogged down the stairs and crossed the road to the hillside steps.

How fast he moved, with such lithe agility for so sturdy a man. His smile had seemed so genuine – as though he was truly glad to see her. And he had asked her to call him 'Del' as Lillis and Allyne did. Had he meant it when he said, "Another time, perhaps?"

Bertha wondered with growing determination how it would feel to have Del Drury look upon her as fondly as he gazed upon Lillis. Bertha had never lacked for dancing partners in Peoria. She received as many flowers as the other girls, even if she hadn't been asked to go driving as often. It wasn't inconceivable that Del Drury might fancy her, under the right circumstances. Wouldn't it feel grand to have Lillis envy her for a change! And wouldn't it enhance her esteem in Lillis' eyes if Del preferred—or at least openly admired—her? Bertha paced the long porch, consumed with her thoughts.

Del jogged through the trees toward the sound of crashing waves. He was short of breath by the time he finally reached their empty beach. Retrieving his watch, Del flipped up the gilded lid to confirm that he was precisely on time.

Would Priscilla meet him here today? Or was their brief love affair to crash and ebb like the clear waves upon the ivory and gray stones? Would jealousy spike her pride? He forsook her for Lillis Friday – how long would Priscilla make him pay for that? Or was his punishment indefinite? Had her virtue overcome her desire?

Del had convinced himself that Priscilla wanted him to make love to her. Her husband had wounded her pride too egregiously to escape retribution; Del was perfectly willing to be the means to the scorned wife's revenge. But perhaps he had misread her – perhaps she had only encouraged him to make her husband jealous… And yet she had seemed so happy for a week's reprieve of the boorish man!

Del watched the dappled glistening of sunlight over water, his hope diminishing as the minutes ticked by. Her step was so light he didn't perceive her approach over the sounds of breaking waves and cawing seagulls. The warmth of her fingers over his jolted Del to awareness of Priscilla's sudden proximity. She pressed a cool, brass object into his palm and Del's heartbeat quickened to feel her room key.

"My maid will leave me at ten o'clock," Priscilla murmured. "I hope you won't keep me waiting long."

Del turned to regard her, but Priscilla already retreated toward the trees; he watched her go with soaring spirits. Del wasn't certain of the degree of her affection or of her intention of prolonging this affair, but he at least felt confident that Priscilla Pruett wanted him to love her tonight.

TEN

Del shifted his weight, settling into a more comfortable repose upon the stone beach. His notebook lay discarded on the blanket beside him. Del hadn't started his novel yet, but he had written dozens of love-struck poems and odes to Priscilla's beauty. She was a rose, a lily – the most exquisite orchid. For three sublime nights she had opened herself to him, let him taste her sweet nectar. His limited experiences had not prepared Del for the heights of pleasure Priscilla showed him. He ached for her, worse than ever now that he knew what he missed and would never again attain – for Priscilla had decreed last night to be their final intimate encounter. Her husband returned today and she would not risk discovery.

"But don't you want him to learn about us?" Del had ventured. "Isn't that partly why we're here?"

"Oh, no," Priscilla had shaken her head, pushing her tousled blonde hair over her shoulders. "This was all for my benefit. I know I've had my revenge – that's enough. If Franklin knew, he'd cast it up to me when I rebuke him. I prefer to retain the high ground."

"Do you still love Franklin?" Del had asked, wishing she wouldn't hide her eyes beneath those long lashes.

"I don't know," she had shrugged. "But why do you ask of my husband on our last night together?"

"Are you in love with me?" Del had demanded between kisses.

"Tonight I am."

Tonight I am – that was the title of one of his most recent poems. They had made love until the rising sun's searing orange rays lit her bedroom walls. And now here he sat, half delirious with exhaustion, staring dreamily at the sun-dappled water's surface, pining for a married woman instead of writing his novel.

"Del!"

He repressed a shudder at her call and rose to his feet; Del would observe the rules of etiquette, even for the woman he least welcomed. Bertha Collins strutted boldly over the stones, her chin proudly aloft and her raspberry lips stretched in smile. She looked so confident of his welcoming smile that Del obliged her. Bertha seemed different today – pretty in her youth. Her smooth, pale skin mitigated the broad forehead and round cheeks; her smile brightened her eyes.

"Good afternoon, Miss Collins."

"You can't ask me to call you 'Del' and go on calling me 'Miss Collins'! Do call me 'Bertha'?"

"Good afternoon, Bertha," he nodded.

"Isn't it?" her smile didn't falter, but Bertha's gaze fell briefly upon his notebook. "Have you been writing? I hope I haven't disturbed you? May I—"

Del snatched up the notebook in swift answer to her unfinished question, wrapping it in the blanket he also gathered.

"I've written nothing fit to be read – and you haven't disturbed me at all. I welcome the distraction."

"In that case—"

"In fact, I was just returning to the hotel. May I accompany you back?"

"Oh," her round cheeks flushed with repressed anger for being so deftly thwarted. "Yes, of course."

Del offered his arm good-naturedly and escorted Bertha from the beach. Priscilla's clutch drew his body into intimate proximity; Allyne floated beside him so gracefully he forgot her feather touch upon his forearm; Bertha's grip vacillated in Jekyll and Hyde fashion. One moment she firmly pulled him forward, leading him impatiently up the wooded path, the next, she let her fingers rest limply over his sleeve, lagging behind him in demure, deferential gait. Del easily distinguished between the gesture correlated to Bertha's true nature and that which she wished to project.

"Allyne told me you were at Princeton," Bertha spoke in one of her deferential postures.

"Yes," Del nodded.

"That's one of the best schools in the country."

"One of them," Del agreed.

"You must be very smart."

"Intelligence is not necessarily a requirement for admission to Princeton, though in my case you're very astute."

"Del!" Bertha giggled – a most unpleasant sound. "You're so funny!"

"I always aim to amuse," Del quipped, relieved to glimpse the hotel's lawn between the trees.

“Will you amuse us at the Island House hop tonight?” Bertha’s Illinois twang mitigated the effect of her flirtatious drawl.

“Is there to be a hop at the Island House Hotel? I had no plan to attend... Of course, if *you’re* there, I really should attend, shouldn’t I? Who else is attending this little hop?”

“Allyne and I are in need of an escort. Lillis might want to ride there with us, or she might go over with Anne and Cassius. Everyone’s going – Kitty and Rob, their cousin, Alva, the Kings, all of their cottage friends.”

“We mustn’t be left out, then.”

“No, we must attend,” Bertha failed to perceive the mockery in his solemn tone. “Will you escort us, then? Allyne and I?”

“It would be my pleasure, Bertha.”

They fell silent as they climbed the steps from lawn to summerhouse, and up the steep hillside to West Bluff Road. Catching her breath as Del escorted her across the road and up the broad porch steps, Bertha found her voice again in the front parlor.

“I’ll see you tomorrow, then? We’re to meet on the porch at nine-thirty.”

“I’ll be counting the hours until then,” Del doffed his boater to her eager eyes before sprinting up the staircase.

He’ll be counting the hours, will he? Bertha’s lips curled triumphantly as she watched Del’s fine figure bound up the stairs and vanish around their corner. He seemed just as eager to escort her and Allyne as he ever had been to see Lillis. He had called her a “welcome distraction” when

Bertha first approached him on the beach. And he had been so gracious—such a gentleman—to offer his arm like that and escort her back to the hotel.

He was a true gentleman; when she met him on the porch tomorrow evening, Del would feel honor bound to drive with her to the hop, even though Allyne had abandoned them. (Allyne would drive there with Cassius Kearney after dinner at Bella Vista, though Del needn't know of this before Friday at nine-thirty.) Lillis would seethe with envy when she saw Bertha arrive at the hop on Del Drury's arm!

Elliott's voice softened by degrees as Daisy's head grew heavier upon his arm. When he skipped a page of her favorite book without inciting protest, he knew his daughter slept. Rising slowly from the window seat cushions, Elliott carried Daisy to bed and tucked her small figure under the summer quilt his mother had sewn for Laura during their first year at Mapleview. Smoothing back her wispy, blonde curls, Elliott pressed a kiss to his daughter's soft forehead.

He paused beside her bed, gazing down upon her five-year-old face, so tranquil in contented sleep. Elliott wondered if Daisy would remember this pink and green quilt and the view of the Straits from her window seat. Would she remember this cottage at all? Perhaps it was best if she didn't.

After checking that Martin and Walter also slept in their shared room across the hall, Elliott descended the narrow staircase in search of his wife. He found Iva huddled upon one of the porch rockers, a knit blanket over her skirts, her hands cradling a steaming teacup.

"May I join you?" Elliott asked, settling upon the neighboring rocker.

"Of course – you're just in time for the sunset."

Even after a week apart, Iva did not seem inclined to converse – at least not during these brief, glorious minutes when the setting sun turned the sky over the water vibrant shades of pink and tangerine. They couldn't see the sun's final descent over the Upper Peninsula from Mapleview's front porch, but still enjoyed the changing colors of the sky. There was no place on earth Elliott would rather watch a sunset – and he had precious few of them left.

"How did you, Daisy and Walter get on while we were away?" Elliott waited until the colors had faded to blush pinks and pale yellows before asking.

"Fine."

"Daisy told me quite a bit about Lily and Angelica Pendleton."

"She adores those girls. I'm afraid of her heartache when we part from them at summer's end, but children that age soon recover and forget the heartache's cause. Agnes was a dear – she had the children over almost every afternoon. It gave me time to sort through things here. I've packed up all of your mother's clutter."

"Clutter?"

"All her little vases and bowls, picture frames and miscellaneous bric-a-brac."

"Why have you packed them away already?" Elliott demanded.

"Did you think to wait and pack the entire house on September 1?" Iva asked scornfully. "It's August 4 – we've less than a month here and there's so much to be done. Besides, I rather like the effect. The rooms seem larger and airier without all that clutter."

"Very well, but don't start packing up the sofas and chairs – we'll still need places to sit for the next four weeks."

"We're not taking any of the furniture," Iva reminded him, her dispassionate tone further vexing Elliott. "Where would we put any of it?"

"Perhaps Laura would like to preserve a few pieces."

"I've already written her – she doesn't."

"You speak of it so calmly."

"Why shouldn't I be calm?"

"It doesn't sadden you – abandoning our furnishings, as if they meant nothing?"

"These furnishings don't mean anything to me," Iva spoke candidly. "This wasn't my childhood cottage. Before this summer, I'd only spent two Julys here—as a guest of your mother—who, incidentally, does not wish to claim any of her cottage furnishings. I know you're sad to be selling Mapleview, but don't also lament its rustic, old furnishings!"

"You're right, of course," Elliott sighed. "We should take the quilts, though – Mother made most of them."

They fell silent to watch the phaeton draw up before Sunset Cottage. In twilight's pale glow, they watched Lillis Halloran glide up the front walk. The man on the back seat sprang to the ground to hand Lillis up to the bench beside the driver. Once the chivalrous young man had regained his seat, the horses surged forward, carrying their young laughter off until it blended with the crickets' symphony.

How many times had Elliott sat on this porch, watching Adelia Halloran flounce into carriages – flitting off to some dance or reception with one of her many friends or beaux? How many times had he been at the reins of that buggy?

"Ah, to be so young and carefree," Iva quipped.

"It reminds me of—" Elliott broke off, recognizing the warning in her tone too late.

"What does it remind you of, Elliott?"

"Our youth," he muttered.

"But we weren't acquainted as youths. Perhaps the scene reminded you of your youth, and how you called for Adelia Halloran? Perhaps you, Hugh and Laura had a similar rig, and the three of you called for Adelia across the street before setting out for a ball or hop? Is that what it reminds you of, Elliott?"

He thought it safest not to answer.

"She called on me," Iva's next revelation further disconcerted him. "Monday afternoon."

Indignation overwhelmed him, rendering Elliott mute – unable to voice even the simplest, obligatory response. What business had Adelia Halloran with his wife? Why had she called on Iva? What had Adelia told her?

"She's very beautiful," Iva remarked. "Don't you think?"

"I suppose."

"You suppose? Don't you remember her beauty? Or were you more attracted to her dazzling wit and sense of humor? Hmm? She *is* funny – she made me laugh, despite my resentment of her presence in this cottage."

"What did you discuss?" Elliott ventured.

"Nothing of substance. I think she called to satisfy her curiosity. She asked after the children and your parents, but I had the notion she wanted a closer study of me – the woman you chose to marry instead of her."

"The woman whose beauty made hers fade from memory," Elliott thought a well-timed compliment in order; he drew a sidelong, appreciative smile from his wife, who sipped her tea before responding.

"I hope that holds true after you see Mrs. Alston again. She delivered an invitation for our entire family to attend her father's seventieth birthday extravaganza."

"Extravaganza?"

"Her word," Iva shrugged. "We're to arrive any time after five o'clock the Tuesday after next. The affair will conclude with a fireworks display."

"Of course it will," Elliott chuckled. "The loudest, longest, most bombastic fireworks display the island has ever seen. It's a good thing Mother's not here to witness it. She'll be surprised to learn that old Paddy Halloran made it to seventy."

"Well," Iva folded the knit blanket before rising from the rocking chair. "I'm off to bed. Are you coming up?"

"Shortly – I'd just like to watch the first stars fill the sky."

Iva unfurled the blanket, tucking it over his legs before leaving him on the porch with his memories and reflections.

Elliott had no wish to celebrate Paddy Halloran's birthday, but he wouldn't keep his family from enjoying the spectacle. There would be music and ice cream, whiskey and cigars, shrieks of laughter and voices raised in engaging conversation. Hugh Pendleton's family would be there – everyone in the Annex would be at Lakeview Cottage a week from Tuesday.

Attending the party meant facing Adelia again – for the first time in ten years. For the last decade, Elliott had carried the image of her heart-shaped face, hazel eyes and glorious coils of auburn hair as the epitome of female beauty. Thought of how he would respond to actual sight of her beauty discomfited Elliott. He was a happily married man, and yet part of him would always love Adelia Halloran.

Elliott had not broken their engagement for any fault of Adelia's. He gave her up for his family; family had always been the entity most important to Elliott. He had striven to fulfill his father's expectations, to be as honorable as old Martin Maier. Elliott could not live with himself if he ruined his father's political aspirations, and marrying the daughter of a whiskey manufacturer was precisely the ruinous element to thwart a Temperance candidate's career. And his mother would have disowned him for marrying a Catholic. Elliott's love for Adelia had never been strong enough to overcome those circumstances.

And now look where they stood! The bank had failed and his father lost his reelection bid all without his marriage to Adelia Halloran. Elliott found himself supporting his once proud and affluent parents and was now compelled to sell the family cottage, while Adelia presided over the island from the grandest cottage on West Bluff.

Adelia had married Elliott's adolescent island rival, Elijah Alston. Eli hailed from Saginaw; his father was a "lumber baron." Eli could have supported Adelia quite well on his inheritance, but his real estate and industrial investments had tripled his net worth. Eli was a millionaire many times over; he was able to shower Adelia in diamonds and Paris gowns, build her mansions and cottages, take her on trips to Europe every year. In short, Eli Alston was a resounding success. How small and pathetic Elliott looked in comparison!

Adelia would sigh with relief for avoiding the fate of being Mrs. Maier, but Elliott distrusted his reaction to her. He still loved Adelia, and he dreaded her perception of his feelings. She would no doubt gloat – perhaps even favor him with a well-deserved jibe. And he would stand beside Iva, hoping his wife did not perceive how Adelia still affected him.

Had Adelia forgiven him – now that she was happily married, with three lovely children and the island's finest cottage? Had she forgiven Elliott for breaking her heart ten years ago? He knew Adelia was not the type of woman to forgive a slight, but how much did their broken engagement still sting? Would she seek vengeance upon their inevitable meeting? Adelia had told Iva there would be fireworks at Paddy Halloran's birthday extravaganza...

"It looks nothing like the ocean," Allyne disputed Cass's observation.

"Surely the expanse of water – how you can't see land beyond the horizon—"

"Have you ever seen the ocean?" Allyne asked scornfully.

"No," Cass shamelessly acknowledged. "But my pa's told me all about it. He always said the Straits reminded him of the coast of County Cork."

"With all due respect to your father, perhaps you should not argue matters of which you have no personal experience."

"Ah – so you've been to County Cork?"

Allyne turned away, not deigning to answer; she found Cass Kearney incredibly annoying. Her gaze lifted to the massive rock formation rising above the treetops called Sugar Loaf. She vaguely remembered learning on the archeological tour that the local Indians thought this rock home to Gitchie Manitou – the great spirit.

"The Odawa and Chippewa think of Mackinac Island as Eden," Cass informed her, unperturbed by Allyne's rebuke. "It's the place of their creation – where their Adam and Eve came into being. They believe it a sacred place. I don't know about all that, but I feel its significance – don't you?"

"Yes," Allyne acknowledged, taking his offered hand to step down from the phaeton.

Lillis, Del, Bertha and Anne had already alighted from their buggy; they milled about Sugar Loaf's base, Del venturing to climb a few feet up its craggy limestone walls. The King carriage rolled to a stop behind the phaetons. Cliff helped his sister, Lily, from the vehicle; their brother, James, clutched his new Kodak box camera as he trailed after his siblings.

In her enthusiasm to greet Lillis and Del, Anne Kearney and the King siblings, Allyne meant to demonstrate her indifference to Cass Kearney. She may have agreed to drive here with him, but didn't want Cass to read too much into her acceptance. He was unrefined, barely educated, Irish and Catholic. He meant nothing to her beyond a pleasant and very fleeting distraction. Yes – he was handsome, and the perfect male height, and a fine dancing partner, but beyond that Allyne cared nothing for Cassius Kearney.

"If you could all face this way!" James King called their attention to his small, black box camera.

Allyne turned with Lillis to face the camera, Cass and Del silent sentinels just behind them. Anne Kearney and Cliff King posed to their left, Lily King and Bertha Collins to their right; Bertha kept stealing sidelong glances at Lillis.

"Hold still!" James admonished. "On three, then – OK?"

"Before we petrify like the rock!" Lily demanded.

"One . . . two . . . three!" James cried.

"Would have been a better photo if one of us had climbed to its peak," Cass remarked.

"To the top of this big rock?" Del chuckled. "That would be some feat."

"I've done it," Cass proclaimed.

"You haven't," Del chided.

"I have so," Cass bristled. "I was nineteen – of course James wasn't following us around with a Kodak back then."

"I bet you couldn't climb it now," Del declared.

"How much?"

"Five dollars."

"Very well," Cass shrugged off his navy blazer. "I don't suppose you'd like to join me? I'll give you ten dollars if you reach the top before I do – which means you'd only owe me a net of five either way."

Chatting with Lillis and Bertha, Allyne paid little heed to Cass and Del's banter, but she took note when they shed their blazers.

"What on earth are you doing?" her demand made Cass and Del pause, glancing back over their shoulders.

"Climbing Sugar Loaf," Cass explained. "We've a wager."

"You can't climb that rock," Allyne scorned. "It's not safe."

"I've climbed it before," Cass informed her.

"You'd – be disturbing the spirits," Allyne appealed to his respect for local culture.

"They've never minded before."

"But – you—" Allyne sputtered at his retreating figure.

How dare he walk away from her like that – completely disregarding her reasonable objections and ignoring her last words! Allyne couldn't decide whether she liked the determined set to Cass's dark eyes, the rare glow coloring his cheeks, how he held his chin arrogantly aloft despite his resolutely clenched jaw. She recognized the expression of Chicago's most prosperous meat packer and the man who would be first to the top of Sugar Loaf or die trying. Cass Kearney wanted to win – in business, in sport, in all of life's contests. Allyne couldn't help admiring Cass's competitive spirit, but his reckless pursuit of victory gave her pause.

"How tall do you think Sugar Loaf is?" she asked Lillis.

"Seventy-five feet," her friend replied promptly.

"How can they climb those steep walls? They'll be killed!" Allyne fretted.

"It's not so steep on the back side," Lillis informed her. "Cass knows; nearly every boy in the Annex has climbed Sugar Loaf at some point. They'll be fine – but who will reach the top first, do you think?"

"Cass," Allyne spoke with certainty.

"He hasn't climbed more than a flight of stairs in seven years," Lillis scoffed. "I'll bet you five dollars Del wins."

"Ooh – what is the wager?" Bertha inserted herself between Allyne and Lillis.

Allyne drifted apart from the others, crossing the clearing for a better view. From this vantage, she saw how one face of Sugar Loaf had more of an angle – very steep, but not vertical. Yet the part Cass and Del now struggled to ascend—just above the tree line—was nearly so. Saplings and other plants grew along the angled cliff. Cass had pulled ahead of Del, but the branch he grasped suddenly uprooted and Cass slid ten feet down the rough limestone surface before reestablishing his grip.

Allyne's heart stopped sometime in the intervening three seconds of his plummet. Her breath caught in her throat as her imagination raced through those three seconds before Cass caught hold of that ledge. What if he banged his head on the rocks as he fell? What if he landed on his head? What if he broke his neck? Or back? Or both of his legs? The legs – she hoped for the legs, for he could survive broken legs. And suddenly Allyne realized how much Cass Kearney's survival meant to her. It meant everything.

Allyne willed Cass up that rock; he would survive – because she needed him. Even if only for this summer on

Mackinac Island, she needed him. She needed his optimism and confidence, his candor and honesty. She needed his admiration and attention. Could Cass really love her as much as his eyes sometimes intimated? Regardless, she must look into those eyes again – he must survive.

Cass scrambled up the craggy rock after Del. He drew closer as they neared the top, Cass being at least four inches taller than Del. Yet Del's lead seemed insurmountable. At their current pace, Cass would not overtake Del in time to reach the top first. Allyne had just resigned herself to ceding the wager to Lillis when Cass's long arm shot forward. He grabbed Del's ankle, gave a vicious tug, and sprang past his startled opponent's sliding figure to reach the summit first.

Allyne smiled to hear his whoop of triumph as Cass raised his arms above Sugar Loaf. Del was the younger, more athletic man, but Cass Kearney found a way to win. He made Allyne think of pioneers, for he exuded that American spirit her grandmothers vaguely hinted that her ancestors had possessed. He was rough and raw and real – and Allyne knew that if he sought to win her heart, he would succeed.

Eleven

Franklin Pruett leaned against the door frame watching Priscilla's preparations. She sat upon the vanity bench, critically surveying her reflection as her maid hovered over her. Minnie stuck a few more pins in Prissy's shining hair before fastening the four-strand pearl choker – so she had brought his anniversary present, after all; Prissy had told him she meant to return it to the jewelers. Franklin watched her dab perfume behind her ears, then lift one of her rouge pots to stain her lips – ever so lightly, as to appear natural. Another pot had some sort of pale gray paste that she used to tint her eyelids. He had always loved observing Priscilla dress, but had not been permitted the privilege much of late. Watching her enhance her beautiful face still fascinated him.

Prissy seemed to be making much effort in tonight's toilette – could she possibly have missed him while he was in the U.P.? And now finally meant to forgive him, as indicated by the pearls? Or was this meticulous amplification of her beauty for another's appreciative eyes?

Priscilla had been cordial since his return from the fishing trip. Something had changed; there had been a subtle shift in their dynamic. Her pride was high as ever, her acrimony lingered, but Prissy's anger had finally abated. Franklin found this departure of wrath concerning.

"You're beautiful," he complimented her when Priscilla finally rose from the dressing table.

"I've invited the Harrises to dine with us," she announced.

"Who?" he frowned.

"Rose and Harland Harris – that handsome young couple from Chicago. Emmeline's befriended their daughters and Francis has taken their son under his wing. Rose has been a saint watching them all while I—" Priscilla faltered. "While you and the boys were away."

Franklin fretted over that pause, but didn't press her about it. He wished she had told him of this invitation earlier so he could have reserved a larger table, but then he was guilty of the same omission.

"I've invited the Maiers to dine with us," he announced.

"How morbid!" Prissy protested. "To dine with the couple whose cottage we're stealing?"

"We are not stealing anything," Franklin bristled. "And I'd like you to meet them – I think you'll like them."

"You do," Priscilla met his eyes for the first time in weeks. "That's evident."

"Yes," Franklin nodded. "Elliott's a good man; I'm sorry he's losing his cottage, but perhaps we could invite them to stay with us next summer? If you find Mrs. Maier agreeable."

"Isn't that rather insulting?" Prissy asked as she pulled her long white gloves up to her elbows. "To invite them back to their house after stealing it from them?"

“Are you trying to provoke me?” Franklin asked hopefully.

“Not at all,” that fleeting glimmer of amusement faded from Priscilla’s meticulously rouged and powdered face. “We can’t snub the Harrises, though.”

“I’m sure the Maiers will be pleased to meet them. Shall we, then?” Franklin opened the hall door for his wife to precede him.

Priscilla paused at the top of the stairs to take his arm, something she hadn’t done since their anniversary ball. Franklin swelled with joy at her rare touch – did this mean he had finally been forgiven? Or—Franklin’s smile faltered as they descended the last few steps—was this affectionate gesture solely for public consumption? Nearly every head in the room turned to admire Priscilla and her revealing blue gown and impressive array of pearls.

“Mr. Harris, Rose,” Prissy greeted the young couple perched upon the settee closest to the staircase. “May I introduce Mr. Pruett?”

“Franklin,” he extended his hand.

“Harland,” the younger man spoke as their hands shook.

“I understand we have you to thank, Mrs. Harris, for taking watch of our children so often while I’ve been away?” Franklin met Rose Harris’s wide brown eyes. “Prissy appreciates all the spare time your selflessness afforded.”

“Oh,” Mrs. Harris’s cheeks flushed as her gaze darted to Priscilla. “It was no trouble; the children are so fond of each other that they amused themselves. And call me ‘Rose’ as Prissy does.”

"You must forgive Franklin," Priscilla's tone was smooth as honey. "He's invited Mr. and Mrs. Maier to dine with us without fair warning, but he assures me you'll like them. I hope you will, or I should feel horrid for the inconvenience."

"No—" Rose stammered. "I mean, don't feel – that is, we're delighted by the prospect of meeting Mr. and Mrs. Maier."

"You're such a dear," Prissy favored the younger woman with indulgent smile before turning her sky blue eyes to her husband. "Where are the Maiers, Franklin?"

Franklin's eyes swept the long parlor crowded with guests. He recognized the white-haired spinster from the archeological tour and that damned young sportsman who always seemed to be ogling Prissy, but he did not see Elliott or Mrs. Maier.

"You told them eight o'clock?" Priscilla's brows rose with the question. "Shall we wait for them on the porch?"

"No," Franklin smiled with relief to see their blond heads rise above the porch steps. "They're here."

Introductions were made, the proper courtesies observed, and the three couples joined the queue inching toward the *Salle à Manger*. Franklin and Priscilla led their procession along the row of white and gold columns spanning the dining room's center. Heads turned to watch their progression, making Franklin feel as though they traversed a very long stage. Beyond their gas-lit path, the faded red walls and high ceilings framed by pine green beams reminded him of a theater's decadent décor. Those gathered around the vast array of tables were dressed as finely as any Broadway audience.

Prissy was in her element, presiding over their table like a benevolent queen. She seemed to get on well with the ladies and charmed their husbands when opportunity arose. Alas, none of her smiles were for Franklin; Priscilla wouldn't even look his way.

Elliott's superior manners engaged Harland Harris, and Franklin turned his attention to the younger man. Harris was a handsome fellow, with dark blue eyes and tawny hair – though not in the same class as his beautiful, buxom wife. Though he answered all of Elliott's questions, Franklin thought Harris's replies too careful. Franklin detected a deceptive note in Harland's smooth tone and recognized concealment in his carefully worded replies. Mrs. Harris lacked her husband's discretion.

"Is your cottage near Brennan Halloran's?" Rose Harris asked Mrs. Maier.

"His parents' cottage is just across the boulevard," Elliott's pale, waifish wife looked pained by the words. "How are you acquainted with Mr. Halloran?"

"Harland befriended Mr. Halloran when they were at Northwestern and he worked with him for a time," Rose volunteered.

"Northwestern?" Elliott turned to Harland with newly formed expression of respect. "What year did you graduate?"

"I was there in '82 and '83," Harland spoke before sipping his wine.

"So Class of '83?" Elliott pressed.

"I didn't graduate," Harland acknowledged, the faintest crimson streaks staining his cheeks.

"That's two years more schooling than I had," Franklin spoke to boost Harris's morale. "My parents were farmers – they thought I was a fool to leave the land for an uncertain future of trees and mines."

"So did mine," Harland's grin seemed wry, almost bitter.

"We showed them, did we not?" Franklin held his wineglass aloft, though Harland Harris's mirrored gesture seemed half-hearted.

Elliott Maier watched Franklin and Harland's toast with well-concealed shame. He had not "showed" his father anything; he had merely done what the old man expected of him. The two men he shared the table with tonight grew up on farms; Elliott was raised in one of Kalamazoo's finest homes. Elliott graduated *cum laude* from the University of Michigan; Franklin Pruett hadn't set foot on a college campus – and yet he had the money to buy Mapleview and its more refined, educated seller needed that money quite desperately. Pruett and Harris were moving up in the world while Elliott fell down a few rungs.

All three gentlemen wore white tie and tails, but their wives revealed their degrees of prosperity. His companions' wives were beautiful, and beautiful women don't often wed paupers. Mrs. Pruett's shimmering blue gown, gleaming pearls and the massive diamonds and sapphires revealed when she removed her gloves were the most obvious statements of the Pruett wealth, but Elliott recognized the subtler signs. Her ash blonde hair had an expensive sheen and she held her chin at an angle only those ensconced in a heavy quilt of prosperity dared. Rose Harris lived up to her name – with rosy cheeks and bright eyes and a face so fresh and lovely. She favored her husband with such grateful, admiring smiles that Elliott thought Harland Harris must also be a man of wealth and stature. Rose may not be adorned in ostentatious jewels and a Parisian gown, but she dressed as well as the finest ladies of Kalamazoo.

Poor Iva did not fare well by comparison. She looked particularly faded beside the brilliant facades of Rose Harris and Priscilla Pruett. Her gown was four years old, though Iva had carefully remade the sleeves and neckline in the current fashion. She wore the three-strand pearl necklace Elliott had given her for their first wedding anniversary; the bank failed the following year and he had been unable to buy jewelry for Iva since those pearls.

Suddenly Iva's pale blue eyes met his – as though she knew what he had been thinking! Elliott was sure their thoughts aligned as Iva's eyes narrowed into reproachful glare. She had been averse to this dinner—at least to their companions—but Iva would never renege. Once she learned Elliott had accepted Pruett's invitation, she felt they must see it through.

Elliott turned from his wife's rebuking expression and that's when he saw her – Adelia Halloran Alston. Her husband held a chair for her at an adjacent table. Sinking gracefully upon the chair, Adelia removed her gloves, set them upon her lap, and lifted her eyes to catch Elliott staring.

Miss Verity Bennett frowned as Polly nodded to the waiter to refill her wineglass – that was her second glass, mind. Verity was chairwoman of the Bennettsville Temperance Society, which Polly knew perfectly well, but Polly cared no more for Verity's aversion to alcohol than she did for her broken heart. Polly really was an insensitive creature. Of course she drank that second glass to impress Patsy Webb and the lofty Lydia Vandermeer. Patsy had been a nice enough girl, but New York had irrevocably corrupted her – or perhaps she drank to dull the effect of Mrs. Vandermeer's ice-cold, blue eyes and grim expression.

Poor Mrs. Collins needed a drink. Verity regretted inviting the woman to dine with them, but compassion had compelled her when she saw Elizabeth Collins, the lone occupant at a table for six. Even doctors approved of spirits to treat certain maladies – if a little wine didn't cure Mrs. Collins's fatigue or alleviate her rheumatism, a little more might make her forget them.

"I'm so looking forward to the horse show," Polly declared, her cheeks like two big apples from the wine, her carrying voice inducing cringes from Lydia Vandermeer and Elizabeth Collins.

"What horse show?" Patsy Webb—also draining her second wine—looked intrigued.

"At the lawn party tonight."

Verity—who, unlike Polly, had bothered to read the programme for tonight's lawn party—knew there would be no horse show. Would pointing this out count as talking to Polly? If she addressed one of the other ladies?

"I saw no mention of a horse show on the programme," Mrs. Vandermeer saved Verity from her dilemma.

"Oh, what a shame," Polly sighed. "They put on a splendid horse show at the '93 lawn party. I've never been to an entertainment like that party. There were games and singers and dancers – and of course the guests danced until sunrise!"

Mrs. Collins looked terrified of this prospect.

"You don't think tonight's will last until dawn?" she asked fretfully. "How on earth am I to stay awake to chaperone Bertha?"

"Don't worry," Patsy patted her hand kindly. "She's with Allyne – Lydia and I will look after her."

Mrs. Vandermeer's thin lips compressed even further at this offer. The older woman—with her diamonds and blue blooded veins prominent under her pale, powdered skin—clearly thought herself Elizabeth Collins's better. In truth, she thought herself above Polly, too. She even acted a trifle superior to Patsy. Of course Lydia respected the Bennett name; it did help to have a town named for your grandfather.

Mrs. Collins's dull nature and uninspiring conversation did nothing to endear her to her dinner companions. Now that she had a stand-in chaperone for her granddaughter, Elizabeth developed a convenient headache after dessert. She excused herself, retreating to her room when her companions set out for the lawn.

The evening's early stars twinkled in a sky still a velvety blue shade. Fireflies lit the dark woods' edge with their fairy light, and paper lanterns dotted the lawn in cheery globes of color. From their vantage at the top of the stairs, Verity observed the party's scope. She saw the bandstand

and dancing square, the lawn games in progress and the dancers performing on the far stage. No horse show or boxing ring, and certainly fewer attendees than the incredible '93 party, but still quite an impressive affair.

"Shall we watch the dancers?" Polly suggested, leading the way down the steps at undignified, exuberant pace.

"We must find our granddaughter first," Mrs. Vandermeer decreed.

"We don't all need to find her," Patsy scoffed. "Anyway, she's there – playing croquet with Miss Collins and Miss Halloran. I'll accompany you to the stage, Polly."

And they flounced off, leaving Verity to console Lydia Vandermeer's justified indignation. Although Lydia's smooth façade revealed nothing, Verity felt her emotion and thought she detected a rare rise of color in Lydia's face, though it was hard to tell in the fading dusk light.

"Do you find Miss Collins a bit… strange?" Verity asked as she and Lydia settled upon a bench to observe the croquet match.

"I find her common," Lydia replied. "Like her grandmother."

"She has an unhealthy preoccupation with that Lillis Halloran."

"Allyne's very fond of Miss Halloran," Lydia acknowledged.

"She's a pretty girl," Verity observed, pausing to watch Lillis' well-struck ball send Bertha's rolling off into the woods.

"I suppose," Lydia allowed. "And her family must be overlooked, for Patsy and I are so glad that Allyne found a friend this summer."

"Miss Halloran can't be held responsible for her family's sins," Verity nodded.

"Their sins?" Lydia frowned, confused.

"Their fortune is built upon the demon liquor," Verity reminded her.

"Oh – yes, they're new money, but I hear their whiskey is of the finest quality. Are you a teetotaler, Miss Bennett?"

"Of course! Aren't you?"

"My ancestors were Dutch, not Puritan."

Lydia's haughty tone rankled Verity, who was rather proud of her Puritan ancestors, but she was somewhat appeased by Lydia's reaction to the unfolding events. Inspired by Lillis, the tall, dark-haired young man drove Allyne's ball into the woods, then hastened after her to help recover it. Lydia stiffened with displeasure and growing unease, her lips drawn and her eyes narrowed.

"Who is that young man who followed your granddaughter into the trees?" Verity asked.

"Cassius Kearney," Lydia spat out the words as if they tasted bitter.

"My – they've been in the woods for some time now," Verity remarked. "Ought someone go after them?"

Lydia rose to her feet just as Allyne and Mr. Kearney finally emerged from the trees to rejoin the game.

"They make a handsome couple," Verity goaded Lydia further.

"They are not a couple," Lydia snapped.

"I'm sorry," Verity demurred. "I just assumed, when I saw them holding hands after some time alone in the woods . . ."

"He's nothing more than an amusing distraction to my granddaughter," Lydia insisted.

Verity thought Lydia deluded, particularly when they followed the younger couples to the bandstand. Allyne danced with Mr. Kearney, then that fine-looking Del Drury, then Kearney again before the "not a couple" stole off into the woods for another tryst.

Del Drury skirted the dancing square—against his better judgment—toward Priscilla. Since he first saw her glide down the staircase on her imposing husband's arm, Del felt great compulsion to speak with her alone – just once more. He had been waiting for the opportunity to ask for her next dance. Not even Franklin Pruett's narrowed eyes and dark scowl dissuaded Del.

"Hello," she smiled up at Del as he waltzed her over the lawn.

"I thought you said you weren't going to tell Franklin about us?"

"I haven't," Priscilla shrugged.

"The way he glares at me…"

"Of course he dislikes you. He—along with most other guests at Grand Hotel—can see that you admire me. Really, darling, we must remember that our time has ended."

"I remember – yet I still had to hold you in my arms and gaze into your eyes one more time."

Priscilla lifted her beautiful eyes to his in poignant glance before turning her head to look over his shoulder.

"You should better attend to your admirers," she chided.

"My admirers?"

"Miss Lillis Halloran and—would you just look at her jealous scowl for me now!—Miss Bertha Collins. I've noticed them vying for your attention all evening."

"I rather like Lillis' company, but Bertha is a growing nuisance. She seems suddenly very determined to win my attention. Last Friday she informed me that she and Allyne were in need of escort to the hop. I hired a buggy, but found only Bertha waiting for me, fretting that Allyne had abandoned her. I've since learned that Bertha knew all along of Allyne's plan to drive to the hop with Cass Kearney."

"Be careful with that one," Priscilla warned through her teasing grin.

"I can handle Miss Collins," Del assured her. "But you, Priscilla – are you content? If I must leave you, then I must be assured of your equanimity."

"Yes, Del, I'm content – or will learn to be."

"Where will you be at three o'clock tomorrow afternoon?"

"No, Del – don't wait for me there. I won't meet you on the beach, but do ask me to dance again before we leave this hotel."

He returned Priscilla to her scowling husband. Del still felt the ghost of her fingers upon his forearm as he strolled across the square, back to where he had left Lillis and Bertha. To Del's dismay, someone whisked Lillis off for a dance just before he reached them. Bertha looked up expectantly, anticipating his dance request, and Del acknowledged his "handling" of Miss Collins could be better managed.

TWELVE

"Oh, Lou," Allyne sighed, her gaze reverting to the massive confection of diamonds sprouting from her slender ring finger. "It's so ostentatious I dare not wear it, but it's so expensive I dare not leave it behind either."

"Do you think I'd flee the island with it if you left it in my care?" Louisa drawled as she pinned the floral and lace festooned hat over her mistress's dark curls.

"No," Allyne acknowledged, meeting her maid's intrigued gray eyes in the dressing table mirror. "The truth is – I don't want to take it off. He placed it on my finger."

"Tell me again how he asked?" Lou closed her eyes to better envision the rapturous tale.

"He led me to the beach – I thought to kiss me again, but then he took hold of both my hands and knelt before me," Allyne let her lids fall and recalled how Cass had looked – his handsome face so pale and earnest in the moonlight. "And he said, 'Miss Allyne Vandermeer, would you honor me with your hand in marriage?' And I gasped – it was so unexpected, you see. So – spontaneous, or so I thought. Not at all like Milton's proposal.

"I meant to refuse him; I had already decided I could never marry Cass Kearney. But then I felt him slip this ring on my finger, and I realized his proposal had not been spontaneous."

"And?" Lou prompted.

"And what?" Allyne frowned.

"And you realized that you loved him?"

"That's hardly something I'd discuss with my maid," Allyne spoke with haughty lift of jaw. "Suffice it to say, he seems genuinely fond of me and it's time I married. I'm twenty-three."

"Your grandmothers will be thrilled," Lou handed Allyne her gloves.

"Oh, don't tease me, Lou!" Allyne clutched her maid's arms, almost stumbling over the shorter woman. "How can I tell them? I must—today—but how can I make them understand?"

"There, there," Lou embraced Allyne. "Your grandmothers love you. They only want you to be happy – so tell them Mr. Kearney makes you happy."

"If only it were that simple," Allyne sighed as she pulled a glove over the glistening diamonds.

Allyne's heart had soared ever since Cass knelt before her on the beach last night with the moon illuminating their faces and giving the pale stones around them a silvery glow. Memory of his enveloping arms and passionate kisses made her flush with longing and joy. And yet – Allyne thought it best not to tell her grandmothers of her happy news until after church and luncheon.

"Will you walk on the porch with me?" she asked as they strolled from the *Salle à Manger* after luncheon.

"I'm not feeling well," Mrs. Webb declared. "We were too late at that party, and then to rise early for church . . ."

"We would all benefit from a little rest," Mrs. Vandermeer declared. "You look pale yourself, Allyne."

"But there's something I must tell you," Allyne insisted.

"What's this? Out with it," Mrs. Vandermeer snapped.

"I can't tell you here – in the middle of the parlor!" Allyne cried.

"Must you be so dramatic?" Mrs. Vandermeer hissed.

"Let's go up to our rooms," Mrs. Webb took Allyne and Lydia Vandermeer's arms and guided them up the slanted staircase.

"Well, Allyne?" Mrs. Vandermeer's icy blue eyes bore into her granddaughter's once they reached the parlor of their suite. "What must you tell us?"

"I'm – engaged," Allyne blurted. "To Cass Kearney."

"Of all the absurd, ridiculous—" Mrs. Vandermeer spat. "Does it amuse you to disturb us? And to keep us from our much needed rest with this – this fool's fancy!"

"It's not a fancy!" Allyne declared, stripping off her left glove to wave the diamonds under her grandmother's flaring nostrils.

"Good gracious!" Mrs. Webb caught Allyne's hand to better admire the diamonds before falling back upon the settee.

"That ostentatious ring only serves as further evidence of the bearer's unacceptability," Mrs. Vandermeer's tone had a note of finality, but Allyne was far from ceding the field.

"I'd think less of a man with more experience of women's jewelry," Allyne paced before the settee. "Anyway, I have accepted his proposal."

"How could you?" Mrs. Webb cried, discarding her hat and pulling at her cloud of white hair. "You've only known him a week!"

"It's been almost two weeks," Allyne protested.

"Oh – two weeks! Well, I'm quite relieved," Mrs. Webb's sarcastic tone stung Allyne; she expected venom from Grandmother Vandermeer, but had hoped for some measure of kindness from Grandmother Webb.

"I've tried a long courtship and it brought me nothing but a broken heart and this!" Allyne waved her scarred left wrist before her grandmothers' indignant eyes.

"He is not suitable," Mrs. Vandermeer maintained.

"He's one of Chicago's most eligible bachelors."

"You are a Vandermeer!"

"My mother was a Webb."

"Is that not equivalent?" Mrs. Webb bristled. "The town might not be named for them, but my ancestors founded Bennettsville, Vermont. The Webbs are one of America's first families."

"It wouldn't matter to me if Cass was born in Ireland like his parents. I love him."

"You loved Milton Jones," Mrs. Vandermeer reminded Allyne.

"Yes – but unlike Milton, Cass returns my love."

"Forgive me for pressing this point, but you were once of the same opinion regarding Milton's affection."

"Ask him yourself. I'm sure—"

"That's irrelevant," Mrs. Vandermeer cut her short. "He is unsuitable."

"I had hoped for your blessing, but I don't need it,"

Allyne blinked back looming tears.

"Be reasonable," Mrs. Webb implored. "He is a Catholic."

"And?" Allyne snapped.

"And how do you expect to marry him? You'd have to convert to marry in his church."

"Then we'll marry in mine," Allyne's defensive mood spurred her hasty reply, though her certainty did not match her tone.

"And your children?" Mrs. Vandermeer's harsh brows shot up. "Will you raise them as little Papists?"

"We haven't discussed our children yet," Allyne quipped.

"But I'm sure you'll have it all settled after your third week of acquaintance," Mrs. Vandermeer spoke waspishly.

"Where will you live?" Mrs. Webb sighed. "Surely you don't intend to live in the Midwest?"

"Certainly not," Allyne felt relieved to placate her grandmothers over one point.

"So he'll move to New York?" Mrs. Webb pushed the matter.

"We haven't—"

"Oh, of course, Patsy—they'll discuss that after four weeks," Mrs. Vandermeer's acid tone made Allyne's already flushed cheeks darken.

"Have you ever known love, Grandmother Vandermeer?" Allyne asked through her spilling tears. "I know you don't love your son, but did you ever love his father? Or did you merely find him *suitable*?"

Allyne spun on her heel and fled the room. She ran down the endless hall—it seemed to go on and on and on—a blur of scarlet and green to her tear-filled eyes. Her heart beat so rapidly she feared it would burst and she couldn't catch her breath until she had rushed through the front doors into the fresh, sun-drenched air.

Not wishing to encounter anyone of her acquaintance, Allyne hastened down the stairs, through the summerhouse and across the lawn. She retraced her steps from last night, when Cass had led her through these woods, and didn't stop until she stood upon the very stones she had floated above when Cass asked her to marry him. Comforted by the memory of his earnest words and eyes, his kisses, and how he had lifted her two feet off the ground like she weighed no more than a child, Allyne felt reassured in her conviction.

Her grandmothers' words rankled because she shared many of their objections. Allyne had no intention of raising "little Papists" or living any further west than Connecticut. Yet now that Cass had declared his love, she had no doubt that he would defer to her wishes in matters so important to her. Her grandmothers were right in one aspect; she ought to discuss these issues with Cass before they started planning the wedding.

Elliott Maier felt like he was seventeen again. For one thing, he hid behind a sprawling spruce. Whenever a carriage descended West Bluff Road, he was forced to retreat to the opposite side of the tree, hoping the nearest cottagers didn't notice the trespasser on their front lawn. For another thing, images of Adelia Halloran filled his mind. And he had not experienced this particular blend of irrational hope and amplified dread since the throes of adolescence.

He had avoided this reckoning long enough—or at least seeing her at Grand Hotel last Saturday had addled his brain enough to make him think his present situation justified. Elliott had decided that he must speak with Adelia prior to Paddy Halloran's birthday party. He needed to see her alone—without her loathsome husband or jolly children or gossip-prone friends. So here he stood vigil behind a spruce, waiting for Adelia to emerge from her cottage.

Elliott had been afraid to see her again, for he had wronged her—and well did he remember Adelia's capacity for wrath. He had broken her proud, generous, passionate heart and he assumed she still felt the sting of his rejection. He expected her to seek vengeance now that she saw him again, and she knew he was selling Mapleview; she knew this might be her last chance. Elliott was prepared to accept her judgment and endure her berating words, but he would not put Iva in the path of Adelia's fury.

He had determined to confront Adelia upon learning of their invitation to her father's birthday party, but seeing her at Grand Hotel had replaced his fear for their inevitable meeting with an almost juvenile anticipation. Adelia hadn't glared at him—her beautiful eyes hadn't looked angry or bitter, though they had every right to be. She had initiated contact—she had called on Iva and invited them to Paddy's party. Adelia wanted to see him again. Elliott had presumed her motive involved berating him for past conduct, but Adelia's eyes last Saturday made him hope for a civil exchange.

After an hour skulking among her neighbors' trees, Elliott finally saw Adelia emerge from Pine Bluff and glide across her lawn toward the dusty road. He rounded the spruce and hastened up the road to meet her.

"Why, Elliott Maier!" she called to him without trace of malice in her tone. "I had hoped to see you eventually—and here you are, lurking just outside my cottage without horse, carriage, wife or child!"

Elliott was sure his cheeks hadn't crimsoned to their current degree since he was seventeen, but he held her even gaze.

"I had hoped for a word with you," he acknowledged.

"Yes—and I've been waiting for a word with you for ten years."

While Iva's evanescent beauty had faded since their wedding day, Adelia's features had crystallized into more exquisite form. Her auburn hair had darkened, her flawless, ivory skin had lost its summer freckles and her eyes were still vibrantly hazel green. Her hourglass figure was not as slim, but still maintained its perfect proportions. Adelia Halloran was still the most beautiful woman Elliott had ever seen—and he had forsaken her and broken both their hearts.

"Do I look much older?" Adelia chided him for staring. "You do – but like most men, your looks have only improved with age. I'm on my way to a friend's daughter's reception at the hotel – will you walk with me? And you can have your 'word,' if you permit me the same courtesy."

"I deserve whatever harsh words you have for me," Elliott bowed his head as he fell into step beside Adelia – how many times had they tread this path together? From the Annex to Grand Hotel, side by side, hands clasped...

"I've no harsh words for you anymore," Adelia spoke graciously. "Eli was always the better match for me – it didn't take me long to realize that. I'd never trade my life with Eli and our children."

"You're not angry with me?" Elliott asked hopefully.

"Heavens, no – it's been ten years!"

"I'm so glad to hear that, Adelia. I never wanted to hurt you."

"Why did you, then?" her sudden question hit Elliott like a punch to the stomach – so abrupt, so direct, never expected; Adelia hadn't changed as much as she claimed since he'd last spoken with her.

"I explained at the time."

"Oh, yes," Adelia's tone turned harsh. "How the Hallorans weren't good enough for the Maiers."

"I said no such thing. It was the connection to spirits. How could my father run for state senate on a temperance ticket if his son married the daughter of Halloran Whiskey?"

"That was it? There was no other reason you broke with me?" Adelia demanded.

"None."

"My," Adelia paused, for they had reached the great porch's west end. "I knew how important your family was to you, but I always assumed you had another reason – my faith, or some other aversion to my character—"

"No," Elliott met her beautiful, hazel eyes. "My obligation to my family preceded my own wishes."

"I'm relieved, but also rather saddened. I never believed familial sacrifice the only reason you jilted me – that you would break your vows and forsake our conception of love for *political ambitions*. But—as I said—it all turned out for the best. I have Eli, and Iva seems a charming woman."

"Why did you call on her at Mapleview?" Elliott asked.

"To invite you to Papa's birthday party. I didn't want you to think I harbored any ill will – and everyone in the Annex will be at Lakeview Cottage Tuesday night."

"You're sure we'd be welcome?"

"Of course! But what of the word you wanted with me, Elliott?"

"I find the words unnecessary after our conversation today."

Elliott bowed over her extended hand, watched Adelia stroll up the porch, and turned away from Grand Hotel. Walking back up West Bluff Road, his relief made his steps buoyant. He had been plagued with guilt for his treatment of Adelia Halloran for so long, and she had finally absolved him today. Her words only confirmed what he saw in her genial eyes and assured tilt of jaw – Adelia was far better off with Eli Alston. Eli provided a finer life for her than Elliott could have managed, and she seemed content. Though he felt a degree of disappointment that Adelia no longer harbored any love for him—or any emotion, so it seemed—Elliott knew her equanimity was for the best. That irrational, barely acknowledged hope he had entertained since Saturday evaporated, but this also filled him with a great sense of relief. He just hoped Paddy and Nora Halloran would be so charitable and forgiving when he saw them Tuesday.

Bertha Collins clutched her handbag upon her lap, her gaze fixed straight ahead as the hired victoria conveyed her up West Bluff Road. She had no appreciation for how brilliantly blue the Straits looked today, nor any interest in the elegant, new Queen Anne cottages lining the road (once they drove past Adelia Alston's Pine Bluff, at any rate). In truth, Bertha didn't really see the trees in her direct line of vision as the open carriage followed the turn inland toward the Annex and Lillis Halloran's cottage. Instead, she saw Lillis sitting beside her; they balanced dainty parasols over their shoulders as the elegant carriage promenaded up Michigan Avenue. She saw the lovely blue and gold bedroom in the Halloran mansion that had been hers for the weekend last winter that Bertha had spent with Lillis and her family. Bertha saw the dashing gentlemen she would dance with at Chicago balls. She saw all of this clearly.

Why couldn't she marry a man from Lillis' social circle? She was pretty, and—more importantly—she was her father's only heir. Bertha brought money to the union, which surely meant more than ephemeral emotions and attractions. Why couldn't she marry as well as Lillis? And have a grand house in the city and a Mackinac Island cottage? Attend all the same balls, receptions and concerts as Lillis? Bertha felt her chances of finding such a man good, but she needed Lillis to introduce her to Chicago's finest society to achieve this feat!

Her invitation seemed in jeopardy over the last week. To her chagrin, Bertha's use of Allyne Vandermeer as an enticement for Lillis seemed to have backfired. Lillis' preference for Allyne was obvious; Bertha suspected they associated without her more often than their little golf trysts and it drove her mad to imagine when and where they met, and what they spoke of… Yet now she need no longer worry about Miss Vandermeer. Allyne was always with her fiancé, Cassius Kearney; she would likely be married by summer's end – she wouldn't be invited to stay at the Halloran mansion, at any rate. That honor would fall to Bertha.

The fortuitous engagement removed not only Allyne from Lillis' companionship, but Bertha's oldest rival for Lillis' attention. Anne Kearney had monopolized Lillis' time at Rosewood until she finally graduated and assumed bosom friend status here on Mackinac as well. Yet since news of the engagement surfaced, Anne was so happy for her brother and enthused to have Allyne for a sister-in-law that she had neglected Lillis. No doubt Lillis felt forsaken, perhaps even a trifle resentful, but she would be cheered by a call from her old school friend. And—Bertha's hands constricted over the bag upon her lap—she hoped Lillis would like her present.

Bertha had been holding the gift in reserve, to be called upon only if necessary. Now she felt it the right time to present Lillis with the token. Allyne and Anne may have abandoned her, but Lillis still had Olive Wheeler and Lily King, her cousin Alva, and half a dozen other old island friends. While initially gracious and welcoming, Bertha had sensed Lillis' withdrawing affection; this only made her more determined to recapture it – to be first in Lillis' regard and friendship. Surely Lillis would be moved by such an intimate gift. She would see that Bertha's friendship was genuine and special; she would invite Bertha to spend a week—maybe two—with her in Chicago this fall.

At last the victoria rolled to a stop before Sunset Cottage. Bertha sneered at the driver's request of payment after he helped her step down from the carriage.

"You'll be paid upon our return to Grand Hotel," she informed him.

"You expect me to wait out here like your personal chauffeur?" the ugly old man demanded indignantly.

"If you want to be paid, I do," Bertha snapped.

"I charge by the quarter hour, just so you know."

"I'm sure I can afford an afternoon of your time."

Feeling her cheeks flush with temper, Bertha slowed her pace up the front walk; Lillis mustn't see her flustered by that loathsome man. Bertha's eyes scanned the front porch before lifting to the second floor windows, glad that no one appeared to have witnessed the undignified exchange. Lillis was generous with her servants; Bertha couldn't see why she bothered being kind to them, but wanted to be viewed by her friend as equally benevolent. Deeming her cheeks returned to their customary pallor, Bertha climbed the porch steps and rapped sharply upon the front door.

The housekeeper—Mrs. Mulligan—answered her summons. Of course the Hallorans had a butler in town, but they balked at such formality on the island. Lillis said they only brought their personal maids and valets, their groom and cook; they hired local girls to clean. Mrs. Mulligan—with her misleading flyaway gray curls and sharp, dark eyes—managed this "minimal" staff and served as butler when required.

"Can I help you?"

"It's Miss Collins – surely you recognize me?" Bertha strove to hide even the smallest sign of irritation. "I'm here to see Miss Halloran."

"Is she expecting you?" the impertinent old creature asked.

"No, but I'm sure she'll be happy to receive me."

"I believe she's out. Would you care to leave your card?"

Bertha unclasped her handbag to withdraw one of her cards when a stampede of footsteps fell upon the landing and charged down the remaining steps. Lillis' 15-year-old brother Patrick chased her, his face contorted with adolescent fury. Lillis whooped with delight, waving what appeared to be a small photograph tauntingly out of her brother's reach.

"Give it back!" he roared.

Lillis stopped so suddenly at the sight of Bertha that Patrick almost bowled her over. He clutched her shoulders for balance, then snatched the photograph and fled back up the stairs.

"Good day, Lillis," Bertha beamed.

"Hello, Bertha. I'm not forgetting some arrangement we had planned, am I?"

"No. I just had a free afternoon and hoped you might, as well. Anne seems so caught up with wedding plans, and of course, Allyne is always with Cass."

Lillis had golfed with Allyne that morning and lunched with Anne, but thought it wise not to mention these activities to her fervent-eyed guest.

"I'm perfectly free at the moment – would you join me on the back porch? Can we please have lemonade, Mrs. Mulligan?"

"I'll bring out a tray," the housekeeper nodded before retreating to the kitchen.

Bertha followed Lillis past the grand staircase, stepping through the arch it formed, across a sunroom and eventually out to the back veranda. What a pleasant place! There were plush cushions upon the settees and chairs, a porch swing and hammock, hanging ferns and pots of scarlet geraniums. Bertha noticed every creature comfort but barely spared a glance for the porch's best attribute – its view. From atop this westernmost edge of Mackinac Island's southwest bluff, Sunset Cottage possessed an unobstructed view of Lake Michigan through the tips of the tree-covered peninsulas. Just now, the afternoon sun reflected off the water in a silvery shimmer.

"What fine gentleman have you convinced to drive you to the hop tonight?" Lillis' chiding smile and dancing jade eyes made Bertha flush.

"I'm still deciding whose offer to accept," she lied smoothly.

"Is one of those offers from Del?" Lillis' lowered lashes and flushed cheeks belied her casual tone.

"No," Bertha knew when only the truth would suffice, but she wouldn't let Del off unscathed. "I've decided I don't fancy Mr. Drury, after all. He'll never be more than a small town secretary."

"I think he'll be a world-famous author," Lillis declared, her dreamy, almost rapturous expression disconcerting her companion.

"Perhaps that's why he neglects you," Bertha's words served their purpose; Lillis' fretful frown encouraged her. "I assumed he spent so much of his time devoted to his first novel, but Allyne tells me he's only composed a handful of poems all summer."

Lillis was relieved from responding when Mrs. Mulligan bustled up the veranda with a lemonade pitcher and glasses balanced upon a gleaming silver try. Even in their "cottage" the Hallorans did everything first class. Not one crystal bowl, Tiffany lamp or china vase escaped Bertha's notice. She admired its etched design as she raised the glass to her lips. Bertha drank lemonade, but she tasted the luxurious indulgence of relaxing on your own veranda, every craving or whim at your fingertips, while your eyes feasted upon a breathtaking landscape.

"This really is the most splendid view," Bertha declared, as though just noticing the grand vista.

"Isn't it?" Lillis agreed, sipping her lemonade until their awkward silence unsettled her. "Do you plan to compete in any of the Field Day contests?"

"Field Day?" Bertha frowned.

"Oh, it's great fun. The whole island participates – there are games and contests and sports. Del sounded interested when I told him about it. He thought he'd volunteer for the Grand Hotel baseball team, as well as the tug-of-war team, tennis matches, and of course, the races. I meant to compete in the egg race and archery contest, but I'd rather watch Del. He'll win everything – he's very athletic. He would have made it to the top of Sugar Loaf first if Cass hadn't cheated."

Bertha had never heard her friend ramble like this. Lillis was always quick of wit and short of speech; she packed a great deal of meaning into her well-chosen words. Yet here she sat with wistful expression, talking about Del Drury as if Bertha actually cared for the subject – talking about him like a woman in love, or at least infatuated. Bertha did not appreciate this potential distraction.

"Do any of your other island friends compete in the Field Day events?" Bertha sought to regain control of their conversation.

"No," Lillis sighed.

"Not even Anne?"

"She did the egg race with me one year – and dropped her egg in about three seconds. None of my friends would join me, but I had Kitty. She always won, of course – Kitty's better than me in everything."

"Why won't Kitty participate this year?"

"Because, you goop, she's married."

"Married women aren't allowed to participate?" Bertha frowned.

"Not when they're with child."

"How long has she been married?"

"Only two months, but she's convinced she's with child. Halloran women have always been indecently fertile."

"Well—" Bertha faltered, slow to conjure response to this immodestly honest speech. "I'll join you in this egg race and whatever other contest you think suitable for a lady to partake of."

"You should," Lillis raised her lemonade glass in salute as if it were a champagne coupe.

"I have a gift for you," Bertha pounced upon Lillis' unguarded repose.

"A gift? My birthday's not until November."

"Yes, I know – November 30. This isn't that sort of gift; it's just something to celebrate our friendship."

Bertha watched her friend closely as she handed Lillis the small box. The prettiest pink flush rose to Lillis' cheeks – was she pleased by the unexpected gift? Or embarrassed? As she hadn't opened it yet, she didn't know that Bertha's gift had no monetary value to fret over. Bertha perched expectantly on the edge of her chair as she watched Lillis' slender fingers untie the red ribbon and lift the box lid.

Lillis' full lips parted, but issued no sound. Bertha thought her friend overwhelmed by emotion, touched by the gift's intimate nature and the sentiment it conveyed. Allyne Vandermeer and Anne Kearney never thought to give such a gift. Bertha felt her chances of being invited to an autumnal sojourn with the Hallorans all but assured.

Thirteen

Del crossed his *T*'s, dotted his *I*'s and punctuated his last sentence with great satisfaction. Finally—a month after determining to write it—he had started his novel. Looking up from the page as he set his pen down, he took inventory of his surroundings as one might look upon their home furnishings after a long journey. Del inhabited another realm when he wrote, but now he was back in his room at Grand Hotel. A mound of cigarette stubs filled the ashtray, his empty glass stood next to his empty bottle of Bordeaux, the lamp still glowed, though the sky beyond his east windows was now a pale, pearlescent blue – and he had ten pages of his first novel stacked neatly between wine and tobacco remnants.

Springing up from his chair, Del experienced a giddy restlessness. His legs felt stiff, his neck and back ached from hunching over the desk all night, but Del's spirits soared with the elation of achievement. He wanted to celebrate the commencement of his masterpiece – and the sun would oblige him in approximately twenty minutes. Filled with a sudden desire to see the sun rising through Arch Rock, Del pulled his Princeton sweater over his dinner shirt, retreated to the bathroom to splash cold water over his face and brush the wine residue from his teeth, and jogged up the long hall.

The sky had lightened considerably by the time he reached Cadotte Avenue. Fearing he would miss it, Del jogged up the hill. His muscles soon strained and his lungs seemed to burn from last night's smoke, but by the time Del sprinted past the old fort, he forgot his fatigue and pain. The exertion took hold of him and propelled him on. Del hadn't any reason to run for years, but he had enjoyed the training in his football days. He carried an imaginary ball as he ran up the woods trail, each tree marking another yard line. The fresh, pine-scented air filled his lungs like a balm. He could have run for miles, but the path ended where the roads met before Arch Rock.

Del was just a minute too late. The sun already hovered above the waterline, casting its amber rays over Bois Blanc Island and bathing Mackinac in its glow. A woman stood upon the arch's southern rise, a sun-gilded figure with golden hair. Del approached cautiously, fearful of startling this goddess of the morning – for her balance upon the limestone arch must be kept. If she so much as wavered, she might slip and fall to the merciless rocks below.

A foreboding of heights took hold of Del – he had never experienced such a fear, but now he felt it keenly. He crept over the craggy stone with the silent stealth of an Indian. Not daring to look down, Del climbed the arch to stand beside Lillis – ready to catch her arm if she made any teetering movement.

"Why didn't you announce your presence?" Lillis questioned him.

"I . . . I didn't want to startle you into any sudden movement."

"But I heard your approach, and would have been frightened of who crept up behind me if we were anywhere other than Mackinac Island."

"Might we . . ." Del tentatively grasped her elbow, "continue this conversation upon firmer ground?"

"What brings you out so early?" she asked, pulling free and flouncing down the rock to the level ground beside the road. Lifting a hand to shield her green eyes from the sun, Lillis watched his tenuous approach.

"It doesn't feel early to me," Del confided. "I've been awake all night writing."

"Your novel?"

"Yes," he nodded. "I've finally started writing in earnest. And yes—before you ask—it's filled with Hallorans."

"As it should be," she grinned, sauntering up the road toward the East Bluff.

"What's your excuse for this appointment with the sunrise?"

"I didn't sleep well," Lillis shrugged. "But I'm glad when I wake before sunrise. Aunt Adelia used to bring me here when I was a girl and I'm still filled with the same wonder I knew then when I stand on the crest of that arch and see the sun rise above the water; it puts things in perspective. I count my blessings and that always mitigates my grievances."

"What grieved you this morning – before the sun's cure?"

"Oh," Lillis glanced away, her cheeks flushing. "Nothing, really. It's just – I overreacted, I'm sure."

Her evasiveness intrigued Del, for he had hitherto known Lillis as a candid lady. He thought her attractive and witty and fun, but she had not managed to intrigue him. He had seen Lillis as a mere bud, while he preferred full, voluptuous blooms like Priscilla Pruett. Now he wondered what brought Miss Lillis Halloran from her bed at dawn – alone, miles from her cottage. Her smooth, serene brow and composed rose lips made him desperate to know to what she had "overreacted."

"What event merited this distress?" Del pressed her.

"Bertha Collins," Lillis spoke darkly.

"What has Miss Collins done?"

"She called on me yesterday and presented me with—" Lillis broke off, a shudder rippling through her narrow shoulders.

"The suspense will surely kill me," Del chided.

"She gave me a hair bracelet."

"A – what?" Del's tone conveyed his revulsion.

"A bracelet made of woven hair – hers and mine."

"That sounds . . . "

"Oh, yes, it does," Lillis agreed. "And that's not the worst of it. I asked her how she obtained my hair to fashion the obscenity and she had no qualms admitting to snipping off a few locks when I fell asleep—ill with fever, mind—in her room at Rosewood Seminary one afternoon. Bertha thinks it a romantic gesture of true friendship. I wish I shared her sentiment, but I can't. She's batty – I don't know what it is, but she wants something from me."

"I've experienced the same sensation when confronting her," Del commiserated.

"She took my hair!" Lillis cried. "I felt so – violated. To be honest, her mere presence on Mackinac Island this summer disconcerts me. Why is she here?"

"She didn't tell you of her plans at school?" Del asked.

"No; she said nothing our last weeks at Rosewood. I thought I had finally escaped her and then I receive her card from Grand Hotel!"

"Escaped her? Did she harass you there – aside from stealing locks of your lovely, golden hair?" Del's words drew a faint blush to Lillis Halloran's smooth cheeks.

"Not overtly, but she seemed stranger the more I knew her. I never especially liked Bertha, but I felt sorry for her. She was the only girl at the seminary from Peoria. She knew no one and had trouble making friends. I was friends with everyone at Rosewood; I thought I could help her by taking up her cause. I invited her to my home in Chicago for a weekend last winter and I'm afraid it went to her head."

"How so?" Del asked, relishing these insights into the mechanisms of the female mind.

"She told everyone at school about it and henceforth claimed to be my bosom friend. Many girls at Rosewood copied my hairstyles and some of my expressions, but Bertha took imitation far beyond flattery. The way she looked at me sometimes, with such intense, unnerving eyes... It was easier—for the few months we had left at school—to let her believe us dear friends. There was no need for an unpleasant confrontation, for I had faith that after our graduation day I would never see Bertha Collins again. And now she's invaded my island sanctuary and given me a bracelet of our entwined hair."

Del turned to meet Lillis' merry, green eyes and they both burst into laughter.

"You're a Halloran – the island's princess. Can't you have Miss Collins banished from your realm?" Del asked through fond grin.

"If only we wielded such power," Lillis sighed. "And I'm not the island princess – that's Kitty."

"I recognize a princess when I see one."

"But you've never seen Kitty before," Lillis maintained. "Oh, you've met her, but only once. Kitty had so many friends and beaux – she was always the center of our generation of cottagers. She's exquisitely beautiful and so smart and just generally perfect. I always wanted to be just like her."

"She's kept you humble," Del observed.

"What do you mean?" Lillis pressed him.

"I don't doubt Bertha and your other Rosewood classmates felt the same sentiment of you – as they imitated your hairstyles and 'expressions.' You were the most beautiful, smart and witty girl among them. All that adoration would have turned your head were it not for your self-comparison to Kitty."

"You're very perceptive," Lillis stopped walking, pivoting to face him. "I think you might be a good writer, after all."

"I appreciate your faith in me."

"So long as you write about Hallorans."

"Who else could I write about after meeting so many of them?"

"Good day, Del."

"Good day?" he reluctantly wrenched his eyes from hers to take in his surroundings; they stood at the foot of Grand Hotel's porch steps.

"This is your stop," Lillis' words recalled his attention to her heart-shaped face.

"My eventual stop, after escorting you home."

"You're the finest gentleman I've ever met," Lillis' declaration thrilled Del. "Is it Princeton manners or Indianapolis charm?"

"A bit of both," Del returned.

They spoke animatedly about the upcoming Field Day competitions as they strolled up West Bluff Road. Traversing the narrow Pontiac's Trail—a short cut from the top of the hill to the Annex—Lillis had to walk in front of him. Each time she turned to glance back at him over her shoulder, Del thought her prettier. Lillis seemed reluctant to let him go when they finally reached Sunset Cottage's front gate; Del was very reluctant to leave her.

Allyne Vandermeer returned Cass Kearney's beaming grin as he extended his hand to help her step into the phaeton. How dear were his crinkled, coffee eyes, the well-sculpted lines of his clean-shaven face, those smiling lips that she had kissed last night? Their arms brushed as she settled beside him on the bench; Allyne felt him crack the reins to prompt the handsome bays forward and the skin beneath her sleeve tingled. She stole many sidelong glances – and her eyes met his return glance almost every time.

"You're more beautiful than this view," Cass declared, guiding the horses onto Cadotte Avenue and prodding them down the hill. "And that's saying something."

"So long as you appreciate it," Allyne smiled coyly, though she shared a similar sentiment regarding his captivating façade.

"Mother wants to host a reception for you at Bella Vista," Cass announced.

"How kind. I should like to meet all of your family's friends."

"Monday afternoon – is that agreeable?"

"Oh – so soon?"

"She wanted everyone to meet you before Paddy Halloran's party."

"Monday is fine," Allyne acquiesced.

"Should you confirm with your grandmothers?"

"No," Allyne imagined how her grandmothers would react to Mrs. Kearney's thick, Irish brogue and tactlessly expressed emotions with a shudder. "They won't attend."

"My mother will want to plan for a day they can attend."

"I didn't say they couldn't; I said they wouldn't."

"They don't approve?" Cass asked, reining the horses in to a slower gait as they descended the steep side street toward the island's southwest shore. "Because I didn't ask their permission first?"

"That's not it," Allyne murmured.

"I wrote to your father."

"You did?"

"I can't claim to be honorable," Cass let the horses rest

when they reached the shore road. "I was hedging my bets – I couldn't wait for his reply, but if he approves, it will be almost as though I had his permission when I asked you."

"I doubt my father will offer any response," Allyne shrugged, hoping her tone sounded less bitter to Cass's ears than it did to her own.

Meeting his eyes, Allyne's stomach constricted and her heartbeat accelerated. He made her feel restless and giddy, and his eyes commiserated with her sentiment. Leaning close—did she move first, or had he?—Allyne's lips brushed his. Cass gathered her closer as their kiss transcended all other sensation.

"Why won't your grandmothers attend my mother's reception?" he asked when they had finally drawn apart and composed themselves.

"Because they're intolerant old snobs."

"They don't approve of me?" Cass demanded in wounded tone.

"It doesn't matter; I don't care what they think," Allyne assured him.

They sat in silence for a minute, listening to the gulls crying over the rhythmic crash of waves upon the stony shore.

"Is it because I'm Irish?" Cass asked, finally cracking the reins over the horses' well-rested rumps. "Because my parents are immigrants?"

"And fifty other things I don't care about."

"Good, because I don't care that you're Dutch – though I'm still reconciling myself to the English half."

"Not English – Scottish."

"Ah – then we're practically cousins!"

Allyne returned his smile, but hers faded first.

"They did bring up some valid questions."

"Who?"

"My grandmothers."

"Such as?"

"You're Catholic."

"Yes," Cass nodded.

"I'm not."

"I'm sure we're not the first Catholic and Protestant to marry."

"I can't be married in a Catholic church – by a priest."

"I'm not particular about where we marry," Cass shrugged. "I understand that's usually left up to the bride's family."

"I won't raise our children as Catholics either," Allyne declared.

"Don't you know it's bad luck to count your chickens before they hatch? But if we're blessed with children, they'll be Catholic, of course."

"I just said—"

"Just the same, I'd care too much for their little souls to let them be heretics. You can teach them of your faith, as well, but they'll be christened and blessed by an ordained priest, and make their communion and confirmation."

"They will not!" Allyne bristled.

"But again – let us not tempt fate by continuing this conversation. If and when we are blessed with children, let us revisit the matter."

"Fine," Allyne acquiesced, but her brow remained furrowed in contemplative frown. She had witnessed the lengths Cass Kearney would travel to win. He was strong-willed and obstinate – had not his persistence won her over, despite her determined resistance? And as demonstrated at Sugar Loaf, he was not above cheating to ensure the victory. Cass was confident of winning because he usually did. How hard would he fight her on this matter if they were "blessed" with a child? She would not back down, but she couldn't imagine him capitulating to her position. Would their first child be the cause of their divorce? And could she actually marry a man she had already considered divorcing? But Catholics didn't believe in divorce. They would probably just separate.

"What of your grandmothers' other 'valid' questions?" Cass ventured.

"That was the main one. Of course they also fretted about where we'll live. We have plenty of time to decide, though we should have it settled before the wedding."

"What is there to decide? We'll live in Chicago."

"I will not live in Chicago!" Allyne cried.

"Darling, be reasonable – my business is in Chicago."

"Reasonable? You accuse me of being unreasonable?"

"Kearney Packing is in Chicago."

"Which is precisely why I desire to live as far from Chicago as possible. Paris is my preference, though I'm amenable to Vienna or London."

"Europe?" Cass chuckled. "You gave me a turn – I thought you were serious!"

"I am perfectly serious."

"We can honeymoon there, but of course we can't live there, Allyne. I am a businessman – I must attend to my business, and that is in Chicago."

"Hire someone to run it for you, or sell it for all I care," Allyne snapped, impatient with his intransigence.

"Sell the business my father built?"

"We won't need it. My father will give us all the money we need, and I'm an heiress. I don't know the exact details – our fortune isn't quite at the Vanderbilt level, but I believe it's close."

"I couldn't live off your father!" Cass sounded appalled as he jerked the reins, drawing the horses to an abrupt halt. "What kind of man do you take me for?"

"Now who's being unreasonable?"

"Don't you understand?" Cass clutched her arm, his dark eyes earnest as they met hers. "I am what I do. I'm the president of Kearney Packing. I employ three hundred men – their livelihoods depend upon Kearney Packing's success, and its success depends upon my management and judgment."

"You'd still own the plant and make the important decisions," Allyne scoffed. "But you wouldn't need to burden yourself with its daily operations."

"It's not a burden; it's my passion. Men need a passion – a reason for being, if you want to be philosophical. Something that yields tangible results, something worthy of his efforts."

"I thought I was your passion?" Allyne asked archly.

"Oh, you are..." Cass tilted her chin up to meet his kiss. "Perhaps 'passion' was not the appropriate word. At any rate, a man needs an occupation, and a man needs to provide for his family – he can't let anyone else fill that roll and still call himself a man."

"But most men don't have wives worth tens of millions of dollars," Allyne drew back from him. "If you want to remain involved with Kearney Packing, I won't stop you – but I will not live in Chicago."

"I can't live anywhere else," Cass maintained.

"You can't? Have you ever tried?"

"That's irrelevant. What is your objection to Chicago? Have you ever been there?"

"No – and that's irrelevant! I will not live in the Midwest!"

"You said your grandmothers were intolerant snobs – the apple doesn't fall far from the tree, I see!"

"I am accustomed to a certain cultural standard that I could never forsake. I'm quite open to any city you prefer, so long as it's east of Connecticut."

"You expect me to walk away from my company because of your prejudice for a city you've never even seen?" Cass bellowed, his patience waning.

"I won't marry a man who's chained to his desk!"

A man like her father – who drifted all day along Wall Street between his office and his club, but endeavored to sneak to and from his home only in the hours Allyne slept. A man who missed her birthday dinners, and forgot holidays. If she wasn't more important to Cass than his meat packing company, Allyne couldn't marry him.

"Do I look 'chained' to you, woman?" Cass waved an arm over their landscape – over the turquoise color of clear water closest to shore, the sapphire shades further out in the Straits, the scarlet roses climbing the trellis before the nearest cottage and the fuchsia hollyhocks lining its fence.

"What did you call me?" Allyne cried with shrill chagrin. "Such – vulgarity!"

"Oh, get off your high horse!"

"How dare you?"

"Allyne, I'm sorry. Won't you calm down—"

"What I will 'get off' of is this buggy! Stop this carriage!"

"Allyne—"

"Stop this carriage at once!"

"I won't let you—"

Allyne dove for the reins; Cass pulled them back from her reach, but the desired result was the same. She sprang from the stationary carriage, managed not to tumble down in an undignified heap, and stalked up the road in a fury.

Her grandmothers were right – oh, she hated to admit it! Only one of the ill bred, lower classes would raise his voice like that and call her "woman." Allyne had only raised her own voice in response to his – he brought out her baser instincts. Her fickle heart had clouded her judgment, weakened her resolve. How could she have been fool enough to think marrying Cass even plausible?

Allyne burst from the woods and sprinted across Grand Hotel's vast lawn. Pausing to catch her breath halfway up the stairs from lawn to summerhouse, Allyne's eyes became transfixed upon her left hand gripping the railing – where the sun's rays reflected off her diamond ring. She recalled Cass's upturned face as he slid this ring over her finger in the moonlight and could not contain her sobbing expression of grief. She had been so happy, for the last two days. Tears filled her eyes, enhancing the diamond's glistening aspects. She did not want to return Cass's ring.

Fourteen

Mrs. Polly Easton tiptoed through their suite's sitting room, dawn's pale light illuminating her path to the central table. She set Verity's gift on the table's center before stealing back to her bedroom. Today was Verity's sixty-first birthday and Polly wasn't one to let forty days of the silent treatment dissuade her from presenting her closest friend with a birthday gift. Polly hoped once Verity beheld her present, she would appreciate the foolish basis of their current dispute and deign to speak to her old friend once more.

Polly felt no guilt or responsibility for their present hostile state, which was entirely of Verity's creation. Her sense of justice gave her the strength to endure her friend's lofty judgment, confident that Verity would eventually come to her senses. Polly had never been accused of excessive emotion. She continued to embrace her days, enthused by their possibilities. Yet even her emotional well could not withstand forty days of being ignored and rebuffed by her dearest, oldest friend.

Believing Verity's stated grievance disproportional and ill founded, Polly attributed another motive to her friend's vehemence. Some flaw of Polly's—long overlooked by her friend—had finally offended Verity beyond endurance.

Polly knew Verity thought her flighty and careless at times, but the disdain exhibited this summer could not have been maintained without some deep, acrimonious root. It hurt Polly that no one living knew her better than Verity and Verity thought her flawed in some egregious manner.

Verity had always been comfortably aware of her superiority. She was a Bennett of Bennettsville and lived in the town's largest home. Her father always had the latest fashionable carriage and her mother the finest gowns. Polly's family were also town founders and numbered among its most prosperous citizens. Content with her own good fortune, Polly had never bothered to challenge Verity's claim as the superior personage. So long as Verity respected her, Polly was glad to let her friend walk upon the high ground.

How had they come to such an impasse – when Verity deemed her no longer worthy of acknowledgement? Did Verity hold her in such contempt that she no longer valued their friendship of so many years? Polly lingered just behind her bedroom door, waiting for Verity to emerge from her room, hoping today they could finally make amends and resume what had until this summer been a wonderful, fulfilling friendship.

At length she heard Verity's plodding feet. They paused halfway across the sitting room and Polly imagined the softening expression in Verity's dark eyes as they fell upon her birthday present. Yet the footsteps swiftly resumed their purposeful pace.

Polly pushed through the door, eager to catch up to her friend, but stopped short to behold the central table. The birthday gift—wrapped in white paper and adorned in red ribbons—still rested upon the table untouched. Verity had seen it and had stalked away, refusing to accept the obligatory gift and peace offering. Her cheeks flushing with blossoming anger, Polly ran through the door and up the long hall. She caught up with Verity at the top of the main stairs, dashing ahead of her to bar her path forward.

"You still won't speak to me?" Polly cried. "After two months of this ridiculous feud! And you won't even accept my birthday gift?"

Verity—wide, mahogany eyes blazing with righteous fury—stepped around her friend. Polly followed her down the sloping steps, staying close enough to ensure her friend heard her fiercely-uttered words.

"If you are willing to forsake fifty-five years of friendship because I told you the truth about Hezekiah Sanderson, God help you! I will no longer subject myself to such petty company. I'll write to John and ask him to book passage home for me; I'll return to Bay City next week. This was our last summer holiday, and good riddance to you, Verity Bennett."

Polly's eyes filled with tears as she retreated back up the steps, for Verity never called out to her, or spoke a word at all.

Miss Allyne Vandermeer trudged up the porch steps. Behind her nearly every island inhabitant and visitor gathered on Grand Hotel's front lawn in celebration of Mackinac's annual Field Day. Even from this height, the whoops and cheers and children's giddy squeals still stung her ears. Allyne had no desire to participate in any of the sports or contests and dreaded encountering Cass. Desperate to discuss her recent rift with Cass, she had only braved the crowds to find Lillis. Unfortunately, she also found Bertha, hovering at Lillis' side like an overzealous chaperone. Recognizing her futile plight, Allyne had retreated to drift in state of forlorn anxiety up the long front porch.

Spectators lined the porch railings for a prime aerial view of the games on the lawn below, but the rocking chairs along the wall were uncharacteristically vacant. Approaching the porch's west end, Allyne recognized Miss Verity Bennett in the very last rocker. The proud spinster had angled the chair to face west, her contemplative gaze fixed upon the Lake Michigan horizon. Allyne turned to retrace her steps—certain Miss Bennett hadn't noticed her—when the older woman called in greeting.

"Won't you join me for a spell, Miss Vandermeer?"

"I—" Allyne hesitated, but had no wish to offend the austere, silver-haired woman. "Of course."

"You look troubled," Miss Bennett observed.

"Is it so obvious?" Allyne murmured, her eyes falling to her lap.

"Some people flounce through life noticing the clouds and birds, but not the person sitting across the table from them or the man they're about to collide with on the sidewalk, but I've always been known for my keen perceptions. I also perceive that you're quite desperate to share your grievance with someone. I've no other pressing matters to attend this afternoon..."

Allyne laughed, blinking back tears as she returned the older woman's kind smile – what a fine sense of humor Miss Bennett possessed!

"I can attest that your perceptions are most keen," Allyne sighed. "And if I could burden you I'd be most grateful."

"What's your trouble, Miss Allyne?"

"Cass—Mr. Cassius Kearney—proposed last weekend."

"Congratulations! I thought I detected a significant bump over your ring finger under that left glove – may I see?"

Allyne tugged off her glove and displayed the ring for Miss Bennett's appraising eyes.

"My, it's lovely – and worth a small fortune, no doubt! But there is some issue?"

"We quarreled earlier this week – he brings out such a base response from me. I'm afraid I raised my voice with his and fought him for the reins; I jumped down from the carriage and stormed away in a huff. He's tried to call twice since, but I've pretended to be out. I accepted his proposal, but I've realized I can't marry him."

"What did you quarrel over? And could it possibly justify breaking an engagement?"

Allyne shared the details of their disagreement and her subsequent conclusions.

"But you knew he was Catholic and lived in Chicago when you accepted his proposal," Miss Bennett pointed out. "Why does it matter now if it didn't then?"

"I was under moonlight's spell – befuddled by this island's fairies," Allyne shrugged, her cheeks flushing scarlet. “What I mean is that I was not thinking rationally at the time.”

“Do you love him?” Miss Bennett’s blunt tone made the question seem so simple, but it never had been for Allyne.

“I thought I did,” Allyne replied at length. “But was it real? I thought I loved Milton – my former fiancé from New York. What I feel for Cass makes me realize I never truly loved Milton, but what if the next man I fall in love with makes me feel the same way about my affection for Cass?”

“What if there is no next man?” Miss Bennett’s question gave Allyne pause. “You’re young – you still believe in infinite possibilities. I’ve learned that more often you only have one chance; you must take it or ever after suffer the consequences of your inaction. That’s not to say you should accept Cassius Kearney or that there won’t be a next man, but you should base your decision on present, tangible circumstances. If he weren’t Catholic and lived in New York – would you still want to marry him? Do you love the man?”

“Yes – yes, I love him, but it doesn’t matter if he won’t leave Chicago and thinks I’ll let my children be Catholics!”

“You’ve got it backwards!” Miss Bennett scorned. “Your love should find a way to overcome those circumstances. I advise you to follow your heart, because you may never have another chance; you may never meet another man worthy of bestowing your affections upon.”

“My own keen perceptiveness deduces you speak from experience,” Allyne ventured. “Will you tell me of him?”

“His name was Hezekiah Sanderson,” Miss Bennett settled back upon her rocking chair, her face animated –

whether with the thought of her old lover or the prospect of storytelling Allyne never could decide. "His family were millers. They had a sawmill, a gristmill – a second cousin had a cider mill just over the mountain. Bennettsville was a small town then; the social classes mixed as they don't today. Though his family were only second generation and mere millers, Hezekiah had a noble character. He was an intelligent and earnest man – and so handsome! Tall, dark, with a smooth, fair complexion . . . his sideburns were rather extravagant for Vermont, but at least he never had those hideous long muttonchops so many men of my day wore."

"You loved Hezekiah?" Allyne asked, caught up in the older woman's tale, imagining her with a tiny, corset-cinched waist and a massive hoop skirt, strolling beside a man in frockcoat and top hat, with "extravagant" sideburns – and a picturesque millwheel turning in the background.

"I'll never know," Miss Bennett sighed tragically. "I never admitted as much – to him, or even to myself. But I think I could have loved him."

"Did he marry someone else?" Allyne asked thoughtlessly.

"He fell at the Second Battle of Bull Run, with Polly's husband, Edward Easton. They were in the same regiment."

"I'm so sorry," Allyne instinctively reached for Verity Bennett's hand, relieved when the woman clasped her fingers rather than recoil from them.

"It was a long time ago – thirty-seven years at the end of this month. The battle lasted for three days, you see; we never knew the exact date either of them fell.

"Hezekiah confessed his regard for me before he enlisted, but I thought him beneath me. I thought I had time to make up my mind, but I didn't. We lost so many good, young men in the war. There was no next man for me. Life is too short and precarious not to appreciate every moment of and learn to accept its blessings when they come your way."

"I agree – on principal, at least," Allyne felt emboldened by the older woman's candid revelations. "But if you feel this way, why have you maintained a grudge against Mrs. Easton all summer? It's been months and still you will not even speak to her?"

"I'll speak to her when she apologizes," Miss Bennett shrugged her rounded, yet still proud shoulders.

"What has she to apologize for?" Allyne ventured.

"She claimed Hezekiah as her beau," Miss Bennett spoke in affronted tone.

"When was this? Before Bull Run, or—"

"Just before we left for Mackinac. I first ventured to Bay City – Polly lives with her son and his family in a lovely, big house there. I stayed three days at John's house before taking the train north. Our last night in Bay City we sat on the veranda and got to reminiscing over all those we'd lost in the war. Polly lamented losing Edward and 'all her beaux.' She claimed Hezekiah once proposed to her. Even after his death she tried to steal him from me!"

"But—" Allyne faltered. "Did he propose to Polly?"

"No! Not seriously, at any rate. She only said it to hurt me."

"Why would she want to hurt you?"

"I can't think why – that's why it wounds me so! Polly was always prettier; she's so tall and slim and graceful. I'll admit she had more admirers. And, of course, she married her man before he died in the war, so at least she has a child and grandchildren. Polly had half a dozen romances before Edward Easton. She wasn't from one of the town's founding families, but she was blonde. That went a long way with the gentlemen of our town, for we had few blondes in Bennettsville.

"Hezekiah was the one thing I had, apart from my family and position as a town leader, I mean. He was my beau, my love – yet Polly had to claim him. She couldn't let me have even one triumph."

"So you're not angry that Hezekiah once proposed to Mrs. Easton, but you're cross with her for telling you of it?" Allyne frowned.

"I—" Miss Bennett's wide, mahogany eyes darted left and right before meeting Allyne's with sheepish gleam. "Yes, that's an accurate summary, Miss Vandermeer."

"But that's—"

"Well, when you frame it like that, yes," Miss Bennett acknowledged. "But she should have considered my feelings. She knows that Hezekiah's memory is near sacred to me. Polly never considers the effect of her words before she blurts them out."

"But she must feel she has nothing to apologize for – if she told you a truth."

"She's leaving," Miss Bennett spoke softly, her tone somber. "Polly's incapable of managing her own affairs, but she's written to her son to arrange earlier transport to Bay City. She's leaving me rather than apologize. She'll sacrifice fifty-five years of friendship to her pride."

"Oh, Miss Bennett—forgive my impertinence—but that is precisely what you are guilty of! Perhaps Mrs. Easton could demonstrate more empathy, but she has done nothing requiring an apology – certainly nothing to warrant your silent condemnation! I'm sure if you explained how and why her words hurt you she would apologize, but if you never explain your position, she'll never understand—"

"Yes, well – perhaps you make a fair point. Shall we both give it a try? If you'll make another attempt with Mr. Kearney, I'll speak to Polly."

"Shall we shake on it?" Allyne grinned, offering her right hand.

Suddenly Allyne realized how brightly the sun shone, how beautifully it glistened off the water, how vast and blue the sky it illuminated. The children's shrieks seemed less shrill and she felt a sudden desire to join the cheering crowds. Maybe she would see Cass playing baseball or engaged in some other sporting endeavor that served to display his tall, lithe figure.

"Thank you so much, Miss Bennett. Thank you for listening, and for your advice. And remember – life is too short and precarious for grudges."

Rising from her rocking chair, Allyne dipped into a slight curtsey before turning to float up the porch in search of Cass.

Franklin Pruett pulled his glove more securely over his left hand, squinting in the hazy afternoon sun to observe Hugh Pendleton wind up for his next pitch. The sky was an optimistic blue over Mackinac Island, enhancing Franklin's joyous mood as his gaze shifted to his son, Monty, crouched with gloved hand aloft – ready for the next ball to come his way. Just past Monty, his second son, Gil, guarded second base, but not so attentively that he missed his father's glance. Gil returned Franklin's grin before they both turned to watch Harland Harris strike out.

In an unexpectedly gracious gesture, Elliott Maier had secured places on the Annex White Stockings baseball team for Franklin and his eldest sons. Back home, Franklin had devoted too much time to his work and mistresses to form friendships with male colleagues. He belonged to Indianapolis's best clubs, but seldom visited them. Franklin hadn't exerted himself (beyond the bedroom) in years. Now he ran and caught and threw and swung a bat and felt as jubilant in the activity as Monty and Gil. The effort was well worth it, for he was part of a team. The other men depended on him to play his part well. Already his future neighbors seemed to accept him, even welcome him. Franklin looked forward to knowing them all better, perhaps even forming a few friendships.

Yet what Franklin most appreciated today was the time spent with his sons. He couldn't remember ever sharing such a close, cohesive moment with them – united in desire to triumph, equally determined to beat their opponents, and thrilled to fight for their goal side-by-side. Monty hadn't scowled at him once since breakfast.

They faced off against a rather impressive team comprised of Grand Hotel guests. Overall the Annex team was superior. Aside from Franklin, Monty and Gil, the Annex team had played together for ten years. But the Grand Hotel team's pitcher was a physical phenom – that very same sportsman whose eyes so often followed Priscilla.

Franklin glanced over his shoulder to observe his wife. Priscilla sat upon the grass, her pristine white skirts gleaming in the sunlight, with an arm around Emmeline's narrow shoulders and a hand resting upon Francis's towheaded curls. So focused on that damned sportsman, Prissy didn't notice her husband's observation. Her gaze seemed intimate, yet dispassionate. Clearly the sportsman was familiar to her and she regarded him fondly, yet Priscilla's cheeks retained their benign pallor and she leaned over Emmeline in relaxed, indifferent posture.

His family was here, together on this glorious island on this sublime day. Franklin had never felt closer to his sons, he had never thought his wife so beautiful, and he had never been part of a team. These men in the field with him today would be his summer companions and neighbors for years—decades—as long as he owned Mapleview Cottage. He had been initiated into their fold, along with his sons. Bolstered by the bond of male camaraderie, Franklin wasn't too disappointed when Del Drury drove the ball fifteen yards past Brennan Halloran's reach to win the game for the hotel team. For once Franklin appreciated the circumstances instead of the outcome and counted his blessings. If Mackinac could not reconcile he and Priscilla, at least it had returned his eldest sons. Franklin was sure a summer at Mapleview would heal his family, or at least mend it.

Elliott Maier strolled beside his wife under the star strewn sky toward the lights of Mapleview Cottage. Hugh had hosted the Annex baseball team to a jolly, raucous dinner – you'd have thought they won the game today. Franklin Pruett and his sons had been particularly boisterous, eager to befriend Elliott's old Annex chums. Gathering clouds of envy and despair hovered over Elliott all evening; he had been relieved to escape Pendleton Pines when Iva announced it was time to depart.

They traversed the dark road in silence, listening to the rustle of leaves dancing in the breeze and the crickets' nightly symphony. After the jangling tack and plodding wheels of a passing carriage traveled far enough up Grand Avenue, Elliott thought he could hear the waves breaking upon the shore below the bluff. There was nothing so peaceful as midnight in Hubbard's Annex – and how few of them remained!

"Are you really so upset over losing a baseball game?" Iva asked softly as they rounded their front corner of neatly -trimmed hydrangea hedge.

"What? No! Of course not," Elliott scoffed.

"Then what troubles you, Elliott? You've been out of sorts all day."

"Field Day was my favorite day of the year," he tried to explain the bittersweet tinge to his emotions. "One year I dared Hugh—paid him, actually—to enter the pole contest. They stuck a five dollar bill at the end of a greased poll extending over the lake. He made it about four feet out before falling. That water is icy even in August; Hugh hated me for at least a week after. And the time Father almost won the cigar race…"

"Your father smoking?" Iva asked incredulously as he opened the front gate for her.

"You didn't have to smoke the cigar – you just had to keep it lit until the finish line," Elliott explained.

"How hard could that be?"

"With people flinging pails of water at you along the way? He only had a small umbrella as a shield, and it was no match for Mrs. Pendleton – Hugh's mother. She drenched him five yards short of the line and Mr. Pendleton won it.

"Laura loved the egg race and always attempted the archery competition. She was still so young when we built Mapleview, she hardly remembers not participating in Field Day.

"Of course my best memories are with the White Stockings. Father and Mr. Pendleton and a few others founded the team. I only spent six short summers with them, but Hugh and the younger half of that team are still my favorite people.

"I wanted Martin and Walter to know that camaraderie and sense of belonging to a community. Franklin and his sons certainly felt it today and I confess I envied them. I wish our sons were old enough to share a few Field Day memories with me."

"Elliott," Iva turned to face him at the foot of the porch steps. "You can still make memories of Field Day with the boys. We might not have Mapleview, but there's nothing stopping us from taking rooms at one of the island hotels."

"It won't be the same," Elliott maintained.

"Nothing ever is," Iva spoke softly, standing on the tips of her toes to press an affectionate kiss to his cheek.

Mrs. Polly Easton bustled about her cheery yellow bedroom, removing garments from the wardrobe to add to her open trunk. A crisp westerly breeze wafted through the room, alleviating some of the afternoon heat. This wasn't real heat – John's last letter described an oppressive heat wave broiling Bay City in ninety-degree temperatures. Mackinac Island—surrounded by the cool Straits water—seldom saw days above seventy-five degrees; Polly hated to leave it! But John would have received her letter by now; he had likely already arranged a return fare for early this coming week. Polly would miss these beautiful vistas and the island's relaxed pace that reminded her of slower times. She would even miss dear little Trinity Episcopal Church; Polly wasn't Episcopalian, but she felt God's presence more on Mackinac Island than any other place she had visited.

A sudden, but decisive knock on her bedroom door made Polly pause.

"Yes? Come in?" she beckoned.

Verity stepped through the door, her large, mahogany eyes meeting Polly's as she took a deep, bosom-heaving breath. Polly waited for her friend to speak first.

"You're packing?" Verity's eyes wavered to the trunk.

"I told you I was leaving."

"Don't go," Verity implored.

"Why not? You don't want to take your meals alone?

Because we have – for the last forty-odd days we've sat across a table from each other without you speaking a word!"

"You wouldn't apologize!" Verity's face reverted to its righteously offended expression.

"I had nothing to apologize for!" Polly snapped. "I told a truth – Hezekiah *did* propose to me!"

"I realize now that you feel this way because I never told you how your 'truth' hurt me. Yes – from your perspective, you told me a truth. But I wondered why? When you knew how much Hezekiah's courtship meant to me. He was my only beau, when you had so many. Why would you keep the 'truth' of his proposal from me for almost forty years and then suddenly reveal it now?"

"Oh, you know how I am!" Polly returned the dress she held to the wardrobe. "I blurt things without thinking. We were talking about the past and I meant to be flippant when you remarked on all the men we lost and I lamented all the beaux I lost. Then when you asked what beaux I lost, I just rattled them off. I forgot for a second that Hezekiah was also your beau. I never spoke of his proposal before because I had no wish to tarnish your memory of him. But that night, after a few glasses of wine, I forgot my well-intentioned omission and blurted out his name. I am sorry about that, but it hardly deserved forty-five days of the silent treatment!"

"I should have spoken to you sooner," Verity acknowledged. "But if you knew how I felt about Hezekiah—enough to consciously conceal the story of his proposal for nearly forty years—surely you knew how hurt I was when you did blurt it out? So why did you wait forty-five days to apologize?"

"I've no good answer to that," Polly shrugged. "Except that now you're appealing to my logic, whereas then you depended on me feeling sensitivities that I lacked."

"Point taken. I should remember that you're an insensitive woman and I should never expect my feelings to be considered."

"You've always thought me insensitive, haven't you?" Polly thought she had found the "flaw" that had most vexed her friend for so many years.

"You're the least sensitive woman I know," Verity declared. "Everything with you is black and white, common sense – you're always so happy, so contented with life that you don't appreciate suffering in others."

"I appreciate real suffering—not the imagined slights of hypersensitive spin—" the flaring anger in Verity's eyes cut Polly off mid speech. "Oh, Ver, I'm sorry."

"Yes, yes – you're so very sorry that I'm a spinster!" Verity cried bitterly.

"Almost every woman our age is a widow or spinster," Polly's tone calmed the antagonistic atmosphere in the sun-filled room. "You'd be married if it weren't for the war – if you could find a man good enough for a Bennett, that is. But even if you turned down a dozen proposals, I wouldn't love or respect you any more than I always have. We've been friends for more than fifty years – you know me better than I know myself."

"No," Verity sighed. "It can't have been fifty years. That would mean we're old."

"You're right," Polly returned her friend's grin. "It hasn't been more than twenty."

"Will you stay, then?" Verity's gaze traveled from open trunk to open wardrobe.

"I don't want to leave," Polly acknowledged.

"I think twenty or so years of friendship is worth preserving," Verity blinked back tears, but met Polly's eyes squarely. "So I hope you'll stay."

"OK," Polly nodded, surprised to feel her own eyes swimming with tears.

"I wonder how crowded the dining room will be after this Field Day event," Verity fretted. "Should we go down earlier than seven today?"

"Yes," Polly agreed. "Those sportsmen will be famished and I foresee long queues for tables in the *Salle à Manger*. Should we venture downstairs at quarter after six?"

"Yes," Verity's somber, yet collaborative expression warmed Polly's cool heart.

She disliked Verity's righteousness and oversensitive nature, but Polly had missed her dear friend's companionship. Verity meant to punish her with drastic displays of temper and Polly resented this. Her nature was too direct; she had no patience for anything less than frank behavior, and no patience for a friend who wanted her to feel chastised and guilty. Yet Polly missed all the intriguing conversations and laughter she and Verity had shared over their fifty-five years of friendship. And she was glad to extend her stay on Mackinac Island.

Fifteen

Shaded by the phaeton's roof, Franklin Pruett drove his family up the bluff road toward the hovering afternoon sun. Six-year-old Francis squirmed between his parents on the front bench. Behind them Monty and Gil exchanged exultant reminisces of the Field Day baseball game over their sister's pink ribbon-festooned straw hat. Franklin's gaze shifted between his wife's pristine profile and the glistening water surrounding Mackinac Island and could not remember the last time he felt so content.

God smiled upon the Hallorans – who had told him this? Brennan Halloran? Or Elliott? At any rate, the Lord saw fit to bestow an absolutely perfect summer day in celebration of Paddy Halloran's seventieth birthday. Franklin felt honored by his invitation to the Halloran patriarch's party. That feeling of camaraderie he had experienced on the baseball field still affected him. Today he would meet all of his future Annex neighbors; Prissy would meet their wives. Priscilla made friends easily – and the Annex ladies would be a far better distraction for her than a certain sportsman.

"Will Arthur be at the party?" Francis asked as Franklin guided the horses up the inland curve, lush, green trees replacing the Straits view.

"I miss Cecily Harris," Emmeline sighed from the back bench. "Why couldn't the Harrises have stayed one more day to go to the party with us? It's my very first party and I haven't a single friend to share it with."

"You'll meet new friends at the party," Franklin declared. "Your future neighbors, who you'll see every summer when we return to Mapleview."

"To where?" Francis asked.

"Mapleview – that's the name of the cottage I've purchased."

"If you've already purchased it, why aren't we staying there now?" Monty inquired.

"So Mr. Maier and his family can enjoy one more summer there," Franklin explained, his formerly euphoric state somewhat tarnished.

"Surely we can think of a better name than Mapleview?" Priscilla challenged her family, effectively diverting their thoughts from the poor Maier family's plight.

"Here we are," Franklin announced, reining in beside the carriage block in front of Lakeview Cottage.

"How pretty!" Emmeline exclaimed. "So much lovelier than the cottage you bought, Papa."

The glorious, gleaming white Queen Anne was thrice the size of Mapleview. Its wraparound porch extended from the rounded end facing the road, along the side of the house looking upon an equally impressive cottage across the lawn, and spanned the home's rear for the Straits view. Today both verandas teamed with revelers observing those filling the velvety lawn between sister cottages.

"Mapleview—or whatever we call it—will be just as lovely after our renovations," Franklin assured his daughter, rather disconcerted to discover her capacity to sound like his wife.

"Mr. Pruett!" a booming, exuberant voice greeted the new arrivals from the porch steps. "And if it isn't the pride of the White Stockings infield!"

Monty and Gil beamed as Brennan Halloran staggered down the steps to shake their hands and slap their scrawny backs.

"Go find the boys—Georgie, Tommy, Morgan—but take your sister to meet my niece, Jennie, on the way – see that blonde girl with the blue dress playing croquet there? And take your younger brother, too. He'll find chaps his own age on the lawn.

"Mrs. Pruett," Brennan suddenly sobered as he bowed to Priscilla. "Your husband is a very lucky man."

"Isn't he?" Priscilla conjured a smile for the jovial drunk.

"Thank you for joining us today to celebrate my father's birthday. I look forward to introducing you and Mr. Pruett to my brothers and sister and anyone you haven't yet become acquainted with."

Priscilla took Brennan's arm to lead their procession up the veranda.

"It's such a shame Mr. and Mrs. Harris couldn't extend their stay to attend your father's birthday party," Priscilla remarked after they had run the gamut, made dozens of introductions, and secured glasses of "Mackinac Island Punch." They took respite among a cluster of chairs overlooking the resplendent vista of golden sky over shimmering water.

"Who?" Brennan frowned.

"Harland Harris and his wife, Rose," Prissy elaborated.

"Catcher on the Grand Hotel team," Franklin offered to relieve the man's blank expression.

"Ah, yes!" Brennan nodded, downing a good portion of the punch – an old Halloran recipe that Franklin suspected contained some of their famous whiskey mixed with the cherry-lemon-champagne sweetened tea. "Poor man."

"Why do you say that?" Franklin asked. "He has a lovely family, who seemed to enjoy their summer holiday immensely."

"Harland's prone to bad luck," Brennan shook his head. "I remember him from the year or two he spent at Northwestern; we were in a few classes together. His parents were humble farmers; they really hadn't the money to send him to college. I did what I could to help—paid him to write my essays, that sort of thing—but he still couldn't afford another year of classes. I talked to Pa, asked him to give Harland a job with Halloran Fine Tobacco and Spirits. He seemed to do well. We knew he was on his way up when he married Rose. Her father owned a big dry goods store – Harland always said she was above him. He knew she could have married better, but she loved him. Why, I couldn't tell you. I went to their wedding—I think. I'm almost sure of it, though I can't remember any details..."

"But why is he 'poor' now?" Priscilla steered Brennan back to things he could remember.

"He lost a lot of money in the Panic," Brennan explained before draining his glass.

"In '96," Franklin answered his wife's questioning expression. "The Bank of Illinois failed. So many Chicago bankers committed suicide in its wake . . . Those were dark times.

"But surely he's recovered by now?" Franklin asked hopefully.

"It doesn't seem so," Brennan shrugged. "He asked me if I could get him another job with the company, but I can't help him now. Pa only listens to Joseph and John these days. Poor fellow seemed so discouraged, but I told him things were bound to improve soon. They can't be that dire, can they? If he could spend three weeks on holiday at Grand Hotel?"

Elliott Maier stepped up to the porch railing, gazing over the Straits as he furtively downed his glass of Mackinac Island Punch. He couldn't help remembering the first time he tasted the heady drink that first summer at Mapleview. His parents were teetotalers; Elliott had not tasted even a sip of ale or wine before his encounter with that Halloran punch. The drink gave him the courage to steal his first kiss from Adelia, but later reduced him to vomiting just beyond his mother's hydrangea hedge.

Now he was fifteen years older—a married man with three children—but Elliott felt like a perpetual boy at Lakeview Cottage. Old Paddy Halloran's red mane had turned a shockingly brilliant white, but his green eyes still twinkled and his ruddy complexion showed few lines. Elliott still towered over the trim, little man, and still felt dwarfed by Paddy's buoyant, forceful personality. He had always liked Adelia's father, but Elliott had been more nervous to encounter him today than he had been that summer afternoon ten years ago when he had asked for Adelia's hand. Paddy was magnanimous today, but Elliott still felt his unspoken chastisement. *I liked you, too*, his twinkling eyes seemed to say, *until you broke her heart.*

Elliott was glad for this brief respite alone on the northwest end of the wraparound porch with his clandestine glass of punch. From this vantage, he had prime view of the glistening waters and tree-covered shores across the Straits. Elliott could also observe Iva's cordial interaction with Hugh's wife, Agnes, and some other Annex ladies. Yet the only face he really saw was Adelia's. Standing here—on her parents' veranda, at her old (if renovated) cottage—Elliott couldn't help loving Adelia as he had for those six summers of lost but cherished youth. She was still the most beautiful woman he had ever seen. And though she was another man's wife, Adelia still inspired admiration and intrigue.

"Maier."

Elliott jerked back from the rail at the unexpected and unwelcome address. His longtime rival and eventual victor held out a full glass of punch in a wary peace offering. Elliott accepted the glass, but found it too humiliating to hold Eli's gaze.

How Elliott had scorned Eli in youth, so confident in his superiority and Adelia's preference. How the tables had turned! Elijah Alston was a millionaire ten times over – successfully managing his father's lumber company and shrewd real estate transactions, investing in new companies as though he had money to spare. He cloaked Adelia in silks and furs and adorned her with diamonds and pearls; he built her a grand cottage while Elliott could not even afford to retain his humble island abode.

"For so many years I wished you'd leave Mapleview," Eli spoke candidly. "Such advantage you had living right across the street from her. Now you're leaving—you've sold Mapleview—and it only saddens me."

"Save your pity," Elliott snapped, emboldened by the Island Punch. "I cannot regret my choice – I don't regret it."

"I'm sure it pains you to acknowledge that I care for Adelia in far greater capacity than you were ever capable of," Eli's triumphant tone grated Elliott's nerves, but he could not deny the truth of his old adversary's assertion.

"Thanks for the punch," Elliott raised his glass in mock salute before striding up the porch and across the lawn to Hugh Pendleton's circle of friends.

In the front garden, Iva held her own among Agnes Pendleton and other neighbors, but Elliott knew she was equally uncomfortable and anxious for this evening to end. He felt more vulnerable and exposed on the Halloran land than he had on the baseball field last Saturday watched by thousands of spectators. Elliott felt all of the curious eyes following his progress across the lawn, judging him. *There goes proud Elliott Maier—he's not so proud now!* Even beside Hugh and his oldest island friends, Elliott remained hypersensitive to the reproachful glances and appraising whispers. *There goes Elliott Maier*—once a young prince of the island, soon to be evicted from its shores.

"Sure an' she's a lofty lass, but she's ours now!" Mrs. Kearney proclaimed, sliding an affectionate arm around Allyne's stiff waist.

Cass's mother, Cathleen—"Cathy" to her friends—introduced Allyne to some of these friends. Cass had inherited his mother's mahogany hair, dark eyes and flawless skin, but he looked so much finer than the rosy-cheeked, plump little woman with the thick Irish brogue. Her clinging arm and lifting voice made Allyne fear for her sobriety.

"That's right," Cathy Kearney nodded to her friend's question. "They're engaged! Never thought I'd see the day! Rob courted Kitty Halloran for years, but Cass never looked twice at a lady that we observed. Of course we're glad now he waited, for our Allyne is a bonny lass, is she not?"

"I thought we had agreed not to tell anyone!" Allyne bristled when she and Cass finally made their escape from his mother and her many friends.

Allyne and Cass had resolved not to announce their engagement until they could agree upon the outstanding matters of religion and primary residence. Yet Mrs. Kearney had introduced her as Cass's fiancée to approximately forty-seven ladies and the sun had yet to set over this beautiful yet wearisome day.

"I'm sorry – I told her not to say anything."

"Not with any conviction or impression, apparently," Allyne snapped.

"Why are you so upset? If we don't marry, you'll never see any of these ladies again. If we do marry, no one will remember the precise timeframe of our formal engagement."

"She's pressuring me by telling everyone we're engaged! And I resent her utter disregard for my wishes. It's either lack of respect or—"

"Or what?"

Allyne averted her eyes, lifting her glass to sample the punch.

"My immigrant mother is too ill-mannered to show discretion – is that what you're thinking?" Cass demanded.

"We explicitly asked her not to tell anyone, but I suppose after indulging in this famous Halloran punch, she can't be held responsible for her words."

"She's happy for me – and she likes you, God knows why! But you're so quick to think the worst of an Irish immigrant—"

"Have I ever spoken against your mother?"

"You told me the fate of your first maid, Bridget – I know what you think of Irish women," Cass spoke scornfully.

"That's not fair! I've no issue with Irish women of *class*. I'm very fond of Lillis, as you know."

"But Irishwomen without class—"

"Why are you so quarrelsome?"

"You started it."

"I most certainly did not!"

"You were upset Mother told a few ladies of our engagement."

"What engagement?" Allyne cried. "We have no formal understanding and the likelihood of reaching one has diminished significantly this evening."

Allyne turned away from Cass, floating across the lawn to ask if she could join Lillis and Bertha's croquet match.

Del Drury strolled through Hubbard's Annex in twilight's dim glow. Fireflies danced over the cottage lawns like whimsical fairies lighting his path to Lakeview Cottage. Laughter and murmured conversation grew more distinct as he approached until he could no longer hear the chirping crickets. Colorful Chinese lanterns—at least fifty—lit the lawn between the two Halloran cottages; another fifty festooned their verandas. He saw her as he stepped through the front gate, her hair reflecting the amber light from the nearest lantern. Leaving Bertha's side, Lillis descended the porch steps and approached with imploring expression.

"Del! I feared you'd forgotten our little party."

"Little?" he offered his arm. "There must be three hundred guests at this 'little' party."

"And that's just the Hallorans," Lillis grinned, taking his arm and propelling him across the lawn.

Del felt Bertha's dark eyes boring into their backs as he swept Lillis away; neither of them spoke until achieving sufficient distance from her jealous watch.

"What's kept you?" Lillis asked. "I counted on you to save me from Bertha, but you don't arrive until nine o'clock?"

"I'm sorry," Del spoke to appease her, though he regretted nothing of his day. The victorious rush of Field Day's sporting triumphs still coursed through him in form of mental inspiration and physical vigor. Aided by several bottles of wine and innumerable cigarettes, Del had produced four additional chapters in the last three days. Much as he wanted to see Lillis and attend a famous Halloran party, Del could not have left his room until finishing that last chapter.

"I was writing," he surprised himself by the admission, but felt reassured by Lillis' complicit expression. "I had to finish the chapter."

"How many chapters does this make?"

"Nine," Del replied, appreciating her lack of reproach.

"As long as it was for a worthy cause . . . As it is, you arrived just in time – and I feel obliged."

Lillis led him across the lantern-lit lawn to Sunset Cottage's veranda, where a fresh bowl of Mackinac Island Punch presided. She filled two glasses, wandering to the porch's far end before offering one to Del. The evening's first stars lit the velvety southeast sky, but pale blue still prevailed upon the west sky above Lake Michigan. The punch hit him with a kick – or was that from Lillis' green eyes gleaming in the lantern's glow?

"I'm glad to be of assistance," Del nodded. "Has Miss Collins been a nuisance all day? Presented you with a hair necklace? Or a brooch made of your toe lint?"

"Toe lint!" Lillis laughed. "Only a writer could think of something so foul!"

"What else am I to think when you say I arrived just in time?"

"I couldn't bear her company another minute," Lillis declared, draining her punch. "She's hovered at my side since her arrival. I couldn't have a word with Kitty or Anne or Allyne without Bertha's obtrusive presence. She'll leave us alone, though."

"How can you be sure?"

"I told her I fancy you," Lillis' smile was rather devilish as her eyes rose to his. "You will help me keep up the pretence, won't you, Del?"

"Oh, I'll put on a good show," Del assured her, reaching up to tuck a stray blonde wisp behind her ear.

She blushed as his finger brushed her cheekbone; Del was better at this, but he appreciated Lillis' efforts.

"You should probably take me driving," Lillis quickly recovered her equanimity. "Back and forth before Grand Hotel's front porch so Bertha is sure to see us and seek other company."

"Would tomorrow afternoon suit you?" Del found himself smiling indulgently upon her vivid, heart-shaped face.

"Call for me at three o'clock," Lillis commanded.

Del's next words were drowned out by the sudden blare of bagpipes piercing the previously peaceful dusk. Forming a semi-circle at the west edge of the lawn between Lakeview and Sunset Cottages, four men played an inspiring, if a trifle mournful tune.

"That's Grandpa, on the far end," Lillis called over the music. "And Papa next to him, then Uncle John and Uncle Brennan. I can't remember the last time I heard them all together like this."

"They're wonderful!" Del declared with genuine conviction. He had never seen anything like this in his sheltered, civilized existence. Their music was powerful and raw – Del heard their notes of pride and familial harmony. The Halloran men—whatever their daily trials and squabbles—were united in their music tonight. Tonight they celebrated the clan patriarch, Paddy Halloran's, seventieth birthday and the land of his birth. Their captivating tune culminated in a sudden burst of fireworks illuminating the night sky over the Straits.

"Your own fireworks show?" Del couldn't help grinning like a boy.

"Grandpa loves fireworks. Come on," Lillis boldly took his hand, leading Del up the veranda. "We'll see them better from the lawn."

She led him to the northern edge of her cottage lawn – over twenty yards from the nearest Chinese lantern. Del felt compelled to take advantage of her contrived opportunity. Their eyes transfixed by the spectacular fireworks display, no one noticed Lillis and Del's stolen kisses.

Except Bertha Collins, who had stealthily woven through the guests milling about the lawn to discretely observe the love-struck couple on the back veranda. Now she watched—fascinated—as Del lifted Lillis' chin to meet his kiss, as Lillis wound her arms around his waist, as he buried his fingers in her silken, golden hair. They would draw back in pretense of watching the fireworks display, but couldn't abstain more than ten seconds before one of them turned to the other for another kiss or caress. Bertha felt a tightness grip her chest as she watched them; she found more effort was required to breathe.

"Bertha!" Elizabeth Collins called thrice before her granddaughter heard her or noticed her presence. "It's time we take our leave."

"But—"

"I'm dreadfully tired and can't leave you here unattended; it's after eleven o'clock, Bertha."

"Yes, all right," Bertha acquiesced in rare acknowledgement of defeat.

With one last glance for the kissing couple at the lawn's shadowy northern edge, Bertha followed her grandmother beneath the red, green and gold Chinese lanterns and through the dispersing revelers to join the queue forming behind the carriage block. Most of the guests—likely those who had only to stumble home to their Annex cottage—stayed to continue the celebration, but at least two dozen others hovered around the front gate awaiting carriages. Bertha thought most of them were returning to East Bluff cottages, but she recognized a few faces from Grand Hotel.

At long last, Bertha sank back upon the seat of a hotel victoria, her arm brushing her grandmother's bony shoulder. They ambled through the trees up Grand Avenue behind an overcrowded phaeton; the boisterous young couples squished along its benches had no care for how far into the woods their voices carried. Their laughter and banter gave Elizabeth and Bertha Collins full leave to converse in normal tones without risk of being overheard, even by their driver. Elizabeth thought the youngsters under the influence of that Halloran punch, which she suspected contained whiskey. But she wasn't offended. The punch reminded her of barn dances back in her courting days. In fact, she was glad for the whiskey's fortification, for it finally gave her the courage to confront her granddaughter.

"I suspect that the 'Mackinac Island Punch' we sampled contained whiskey – I certainly hope whiskey is the culprit for your embarrassing conduct today."

"What?" Bertha cried, her hackles rising.

"You trailed after poor Miss Halloran like her lapdog! When it was clear she wished to be free of you."

"She did not."

"She did, Bertha! This was her grandfather's party. She knew every guest in attendance and was obliged to speak with them all – and she did not appreciate you hovering at her elbow so that she had to introduce you thirty times! Have you no sense of decency? I certainly raised you to have better manners. You are the daughter of Peoria's most prominent citizen and a state senator – have some self respect!"

"I hope whiskey is the culprit for your rude words!" Bertha returned. "Lillis offered to introduce me to more of her island friends – that is why I accompanied her."

"And when all the guests had arrived, after your first croquet game—when it was quite evident Miss Vandermeer sought a private word with Miss Halloran—you refused to retreat. The poor girl practically ran into Mr. Drury's arms when he arrived, and still you followed her! Why, Bertha? What is this— obsession— with Lillis Halloran?"

"It's not an obsession," Bertha snapped. "Lillis is my dearest friend. And I believe she'll invite me to spend a week or two with her in Chicago this fall. Think how I could benefit from two weeks in Chicago!"

"How, Bertha? How would you 'benefit' from two weeks in Chicago?"

"I'd be introduced to so many eligible young men – far more promising prospects than I could ever find in Peoria."

"Peoria has plenty of fine—"

"I want better than Peoria," Bertha cut her short, her eyes lifting to the stars over Mackinac Island as their victoria split from the phaeton, emerging from the trees at the top of West Bluff Road. "I want Chicago – the biggest, most exciting city in the entire Midwest. I want a big house on Michigan Avenue like the Hallorans and a cottage on Mackinac."

"My! You want a lot from these two weeks that may not even transpire!"

"They will," Bertha declared, her tone bold and confident. "I'll make it happen."

"But what if Lillis doesn't ask you—"

"She will," Bertha insisted. "I worried, for awhile there... Lillis seemed to prefer Allyne's company. But Allyne will likely be Mrs. Kearney by the fall – maybe even living in New York or Europe. And Lillis will want an autumn diversion. She bores so easily. She's always after new places and faces – Lillis detests custom and routine. With Kitty newly married, Anne Kearney helping Allyne make wedding plans, that annoying Olive Wheeler back in Kalamazoo and Alva back at school, Lillis will be bored to tears."

"What of Mr. Drury?" Elizabeth asked warily.

"Lillis doesn't really fancy him," Bertha scoffed. "He's a no account writer with no published works who lives in Indianapolis."

"You told me he's a Princeton man, acquainted with Miss Vandermeer."

"Yes, but there's no money. His tails are at least ten years old – probably his father's. Del Drury is nothing more than Lillis' present distraction; she'll forget all about him when she returns to Chicago and he to Indiana."

"You're putting too much faith in another person," Elizabeth tried a different tactic. "Even if Lillis would like to invite you to Chicago, a dozen factors might thwart her."

"Why must you be disagreeable?" Bertha snapped as their carriage rumbled beside Grand Hotel's front porch, rolling to a stop beneath the central portico. "Lillis will ask me to stay – you'll see."

Elizabeth watched her granddaughter stomp up the porch steps with furrowed brow. Bertha's determination felt dangerous; she was so confident of events unfolding as she wished them to, but Elizabeth very much doubted a Halloran invitation forthcoming. She masked it behind a comely façade and sweet smile, but Elizabeth had still sensed Lillis Halloran's wary regard for Bertha. Lillis' aversion to Bertha went beyond disdain; despite her self-confidence and poise, the Halloran girl seemed almost apprehensive of Bertha. Elizabeth feared her granddaughter's reaction when that invitation to Chicago failed to materialize.

Sixteen

The day started like any other – sun rising over Lake Huron, sky brilliant blue, air crisp like a fall morning in Indianapolis, though it was only August 22. Franklin Pruett and his family occupied the round table by the first window; the dining room staff had taken to reserving this particular table for the Pruetts (they were well compensated for their efforts). Monty and Gil bent their heads together, planning today's adventure. Emmeline stared out the window, smiling upon the majestic view of sapphire water under fair sky. Prissy fussed over Francis, tucking his napkin over his knickers.

Franklin unfurled yesterday's edition of the *Chicago Tribune* as the waiter circled the table pouring coffee for he and Priscilla and milk for the children. Monty requested coffee; his twisted, repulsed expression upon taste of the bitter drink made Franklin chuckle before returning his focus to the headlines. A hurricane had destroyed an entire city on North Carolina's Outer Banks, President McKinley advocated the gold standard, and a sensational murder rampage shocked even those jaded Chicagoans. Franklin read the names twice before digesting their significance.

"Monty, Gil," Franklin waited until his older sons had finished their breakfasts before making the request. "Will you take Emmeline and Francis on a drive? I require your mother's attention, but no one else should miss out on this fine day."

"What's wrong?" Priscilla asked as they waved their children off, Monty at the reins of a rented buggy.

Franklin took her elbow, guiding his wife up the porch steps and several yards along its western half to a pair of vacant rockers. He handed Priscilla the newspaper, admiring her thick lashes lowered to read and the rosy flush coloring her cheeks. Her narrow shoulders shook, and when her sky blue eyes lifted to his, they swam with tears.

The article detailed the gruesome murder of a beautiful young woman and her three children. Murders in tenements involving the primitive passions of immigrants seldom garnered note in the papers, but when a handsome, wholesome, blue-eyed American murders his wholesome, blonde wife and their three towheaded, cherubic children, the *Tribune* took notice.

"I can't believe it," Priscilla murmured. "They seemed like the perfect couple. Rose was so beautiful and Harland seemed to worship her. And those beautiful children – " Priscilla choked on a sob. "What if Emmeline reads of this? What if she reads about how her new friends—Juliet and Cecilia—were stabbed to death by their own father? Can we tell Francis that his friend, Arthur, had his throat sliced—"

"Stop," Franklin drew his wife up from the rocking chair and into his arms, holding her until her rapid breaths slowed to normal cadence.

"I envied Rose Harris," Priscilla spoke softly, drifting down the porch toward the curved western railing. "Not for her youth or beauty, but I envied her happiness. She looked upon her husband with such pride and love – I envied her that."

"I envied Harland for the same reason," Franklin acknowledged. "I think that's why he killed them. You heard what Brennan Halloran told us – Rose's father owned a big dry goods store in Chicago. She grew up prosperous, and she was beautiful – Harland definitely married up. But he'd lost so much in the Panic, and he never recovered. The paper said he was broke; their house had gone into foreclosure. And he couldn't bear to see the love and pride fade from his wife's eyes. He couldn't let her learn of his failure."

"Promise if you ever lose our money, you won't murder me?" Priscilla spoke in mock-serious tone. "I'll forgive you for it and we'll make do. But if you ever hurt the children—"

"Good God, Prissy! How can you even think I would harm our children?"

"Well, you've given Monty a fair amount of the strap, though he always did earn his punishments. I'm sorry – I'm still in shock. Of course I know you'd never hurt the children. Though poor Rose Harris likely thought the same of Harland..."

"You would forgive me for bankrupting the family, but not for my actual transgressions?" Franklin watched her closely, almost holding his breath as he awaited her response.

"I forgive you," Priscilla's beautiful eyes finally lifted to his. "This morning I made up my mind to tell you that I intend to endeavor to return to civility, for the children. But now…"

Franklin waited, his chest inflating with hope as Priscilla blinked back looming tears.

"Now I think I mean it. For so long, I've compared myself to others. I made assumptions; I always assumed others were happier than me, while I smiled like my own life was the pink of perfection. I was so angry with you, so humiliated when we first arrived on Mackinac. And then I saw the Harrises with their fond smiles and well-behaved children in matching clothes—how wrong my assumptions about them proved to be! It's made me realize—there is no perfect family or life or marriage.

"Oh, Franklin," Priscilla reached for his hands. "I know why you sought those other women. I can't judge you for that when my refusal drove you to their arms. My pride suffered the cruelest blow. And after what I've just read in that paper – how ridiculous to let wounded pride tear this family apart! I don't want to do that, Franklin. I love our family – I couldn't be happier with any other."

"I had the same thought as I watched the Northern Lights – that we should stay together for our children. And even if you glared at me every day and never forgave me, we'd put on a good show for the kids, because they're the most important thing for both of us. But oh, Priscilla – your forgiveness heartens me. I've always loved you and always will, and I hope some day to win your love back."

"You're perfectly welcome to try," Priscilla returned his smile for the first time this summer.

Miss Allyne Vandermeer rocked absently back and forth, her frowning gaze fixed upon some point of the Lower Peninsula's tree-lined shore. She thought of Milton and Josie, vaguely wondering where in this small world they might be. One of her New York "friends" had enclosed a description of their wedding from *Town Topics*. "The beautiful Miss Van Buhler" – ha! Josie was hardly a beauty. Allyne believed every detail of Josie's sumptuous gown and elaborate veil, but calling her 'beautiful' was decidedly yellow journalism.

Josie had always wanted to best Allyne. Her fortune was greater, but Josie had never managed to surpass her best friend in appearance, wit or agility. So she bought Allyne's fiancé. Josie turned out to be a good friend (though quite unintentionally), for she had saved Allyne from marriage to Milton Jones. To think he had once made her heart flutter, had once made her weep wretchedly – that she had attempted to end her life if she could not live with Milton! Now the thought of him filled her with indifferent disdain and a sense of profound relief not to be tied to him.

Now Cass Kearney made her heart flutter, and he made her weep. But the experience was entirely different from Allyne's first broken heart. With Milton, she had loved how he made her feel, gloried in the pride of strolling beside the most handsome man in New York and the envious glances her connection to him garnered. When he jilted her, she wept for her humiliation, her sense of betrayal. She had cried for herself—poor Allyne—but her present misery had nothing to do with her feelings. She only thought of Cass. Was he sad, morose? Did he miss her? Had her harsh words hurt him? Or made him realize they were ill suited? Would he bother with her after their latest spat? Or would he look out over the Straits and be as relieved to be rid of her as she was to be free from Milton?

Tears rolled down Allyne's pale cheeks; she didn't want Cass to be sad, but she didn't want him to feel relieved to be free of her. If she were honest, she wanted him to suffer an eternity of regret and misery if he forsook her. Allyne was accustomed to people forsaking her – her mother in death, her father to his office, her best friend and fiancé (that had been a team effort), several nurses, and a slut maid. Cass was bound to abandon her, too; Allyne wasn't capable of inspiring love or loyalty, or even nominal affection.

So wrapped up in her fierce thoughts and torrid emotion, Allyne hadn't noticed the tall man's approach. His lank figure blocked the sun, casting her face in shadow, but Allyne took no note of him until he called her name. Then her heavy-lidded eyes widened with shock of recognition – what was her father doing on Mackinac Island?

Del Drury sat slumped over his desk, pen in hand, hovering above the same blank sheet of paper he had been staring at for three days. It was no use. His hero and heroine, their lives, their dramas – he could scarcely recall where they lived. He had no idea where his novel should venture. He couldn't write a single sentence remotely pertaining to the characters he had been so enthusiastic for just four days ago. Del had been unable to write since Paddy Halloran's birthday party.

Thoughts of Lillis consumed him, blotting out all else. His book? A trivial pastime. Priscilla? Already consigned to a fond memory. His dwindling finances? Not worth fretting over while he could still afford his room at Grand Hotel.

When Del wasn't thinking of Lillis he pondered why he thought of Lillis. She was beautiful, but not striking like Priscilla. Lillis didn't inspire Del to write poetry, but he could not think of anyone he would rather read a poem to. She was fearless; Del thought he could tell her anything and she wouldn't be shocked. Perhaps some of her mystique derived from her Halloran connection. She was part of that jolly clan who presided like royalty over island society. Lillis would be the first to scoff at the label, but she really was a little princess – a devilish, slightly wicked princess, but still a princess.

"Oh, God," Del let his forehead drop to rest upon the blank page. "I have to see her again or I'll go crazy."

He hadn't seen Lillis since the day after Paddy Halloran's party. Del hadn't forgotten her request to take her for a drive and had called for her promptly at three o'clock. He felt ashamed now for his behavior Wednesday afternoon. Del had embarked upon the drive as a man fulfilling an unwelcome duty. He had a novel to write and chastised himself for succumbing to green eyes under Chinese lanterns. Lillis had quickly sensed his sudden reserve and asked him to drive her to her Aunt Adelia's cottage. Her infectious charm had lifted his spirits in the short time it took to reach Pine Bluff, but then Lillis slipped away just as Del had decided he wanted her company.

With some of his meager remaining funds, Del rented another small phaeton and drove recklessly to Sunset Cottage. He strode up the front walk, full of purpose that suddenly dissolved under the sharp, blue eyes of the Halloran housekeeper.

"Mrs. Mulligan," Del removed his hat. "Is Miss Halloran in?"

"Wait here," the short, stout woman invited him into the vast front parlor before bustling off in search of Lillis. She returned within minutes to inform him that Miss Halloran was not at home.

"Oh, yes – she is!" a rich voice carried from the veranda.

Del followed the voice to the porch; Kitty's arm circled Lillis' slender waist, propelling her younger sister forward.

"Lillis," he smiled sheepishly in greeting.

"Del," Lillis addressed him through narrowed eyes.

"Would you – go for a drive with me?" Del ventured.

Lillis hesitated, her jade eyes speculative, considering – hopeful, yet wary.

"Yes, she'll go," Kitty practically flung her sister into Del's arms. "You'll be a gentleman, of course?"

"Of course," Del nodded gravely.

"Because if you aren't, you'll be driven off this island – never permitted to return."

"Good gracious, Kitty!" Lillis cried, snatching Del's arm and marching him up the front walk to the waiting two-seat phaeton.

They drove in silence through the Annex, then inland through the woods along narrow, Queen Anne's Lace-lined roads. Del kept waiting for Lillis to speak – she usually initiated their dialogue. Her silence intrigued him and made him desperate for her thoughts. Concentrating on reining in the horses as they descended the curving lane, Del let them fall into a measured plod along the shore road. Turning his gaze from pale, turquoise water to Lillis' serene profile, Del shed all reserve.

"I'm sorry for being such a bounder on Wednesday."

"Why were you, though?" Lillis asked, her tone more serious, harsher than he had ever heard it.

"I was consumed with my novel; I thought you distracted me from my writing."

"I should hope I distract you in some fashion," Lillis proclaimed.

"You do – that's why I'm here. I realized I'd rather be with you than write. In fact, you make me question the entire premise of the novel."

"Do I have such an affect?"

Del couldn't resist Lillis' twinkling eyes; he dropped the reins as his hands rose to cradle her face. Today they kissed under the sun, in the sobriety of midday. And yet her lips were as sweet and supple and enthusiastic as they had been at Paddy's party.

"Good heavens," Lillis drew back, her cheeks flushing scarlet as she turned her gaze to the water.

"I love you," Del blurted. "I didn't mean to fall in love with you, and I'm not worthy of you."

"Don't say that," Lillis clasped his hands.

"I'm not," Del insisted. "I am working on a novel, but I've only ever had a few short stories published. I might make a success of it, but I haven't yet. I'm not worthy of your hand."

"I've read your *Scribner's* essay – you've real talent, Del. You'll succeed."

She really thought so, and her confidence bolstered Del's spirits. He was a damned good writer; he would rework his novel, start over – make it even better. The heroine's eyes would be changed from sky blue to jade green. She would be a New Woman – who golfed and rode a bicycle up hills that winded other mortals, a young suffragette without the anger, a princess with a wicked sense of humor.

"Lillis," still holding her hands, Del met her eyes with earnest expression. "Would you wait for me? Not indefinitely – but until I have a novel published and the means to marry you?"

"Is this a proposal?" Lillis' thin, tawny brows rose.

"I can't ask you to marry me until I'm worthy. I would never bind you with commitment until I've earned it. But if you could give me a year—six months at least—"

"I'll only agree to turn my numerous admirers in Chicago away if we're engaged."

"But what if I can't get my novel published? I'm near penniless – you don't want the sordidness of a broken engagement. It might put off your numerous admirers in the unlikely event my novel's not a raging success."

"You claim to be a writer and yet cannot see the simplest solution! It would be a *secret* engagement. Secret engagements figure in four out of ten novels, in my experience. Perhaps I spoke hastily before. I'm not sure you'll make it, after all."

Del drew her into his arms, kissing her through his laughter. *God, he loved this woman!*

"Secretly engaged," he drew back and cracked the reins, urging the old horse up the shore road. "Will you be at the hotel ball tonight?"

"Of course – it's in honor of our secret engagement, didn't you know? But we won't tell anyone."

"No one."

"Oh, but I have to tell Allyne."

"Why Allyne? Why not Kitty or Anne?" Del wondered.

"Because she's from New York; she won't feel compelled to tell anyone else in Chicago. And I will have to tell at least one person or burst."

"You can't keep a secret for two weeks?" Del chided. "Isn't Allyne going back to New York in September?"

"No; she'll be staying with my family in Chicago so she can be closer to Cass."

"Is their engagement still on?"

"It might be off again seven times between now and their wedding day, but I have no doubt they'll marry. They're perfect for each other. His confidence makes up for her uncertainty, and she softens him – I've never seen Cass so kind and sensitive to others. She's a poor little drifter with no real family; Cass is from a tight-knit, affectionate clan who will embrace her and laugh at her haughty airs. There's so much more to Allyne than her friends and family in New York let her reveal; Cass encourages her."

"As always, I'm impressed by your perceptions. Only knowing her this summer, you wouldn't recognize the Allyne I knew in New York."

"How so?" Lillis asked.

"New York society is very competitive," Del explained. "There are many different levels and sets. Allyne was definitely of the top set, but not one of its most preeminent members. Yet she was just pretty enough and just wealthy enough for the other young ladies of her set to see her as a potential threat to their dominance. I'm afraid she was rather cowed in their presence."

"And it's not as though her father instilled any pride in her," Lillis spoke resentfully.

"Exactly. You would have torn those girls to shreds, but Allyne believed every nasty thing they said about her. She was timid, subdued – so scared of doing the wrong thing, so eager to please everyone . . . The ladies let up a bit when Milton removed Allyne as a source of competition."

"Milton – her fiancé? Allyne's friends weren't envious?"

"No one else thought him much of a catch. His old name wasn't quite enough to compensate for his lack of fortune, though his good looks kept him on every invitation list."

"Josie Van Buhler thought Milton a 'catch.'"

"I can't speak to Miss Van Buhler's betrayal of her closest friend, but I can definitively state that the only reason Milton jilted Allyne for Josie was an additional ten million dollars of net worth."

"How do you know this?" Lillis asked.

"I've seen pigs I'd rather kiss than Josie Van Buhler. Trust me – no man would choose her over Allyne for any less than ten mill."

"Does Allyne know that?"

"I should think it was obvious," Del shrugged.

"Would you tell her, though? I don't think it was ever obvious to her."

"OK," Del nodded, leaning over to steal a swift, yet delicious kiss. "But enough about Allyne. I want to know more about our secret engagement . . ."

Seventeen

"Would you walk with me, Allyne?" Randolph Vandermeer asked his daughter as they strolled from the *Salle à Manger* Saturday afternoon.

Allyne nodded, wishing her grandmothers a good nap before leading her father out the front doors, across the road and down the steps. She didn't pause at the summerhouse, or beside the croquet games in progress on the lawn. Her father didn't question her as she led him through the woods and finally to the stone-covered beach with prime view of the two peninsula tips stretching longingly toward each other over the sapphire water.

"This is where Cass proposed," she told her father in timid, yet antagonistic tone.

"Do you not think your acceptance a bit hasty?" her father asked, straining to contain the volume of his voice. "You had only been acquainted with him for two weeks."

"Is that what Grandmother Vandermeer said?" Allyne cried defensively.

"That is merely a fact of date and time," her father replied with maddening practicality.

"You needn't have come all the way to Michigan," Allyne strove to keep overwhelming emotion from infecting her tone. “I’m perfectly aware of how long we’ve known each other, and I know him better after a month than I knew Milton or Josie after years of acquaintance.”

“I knew the second time I saw your mother.”

Randolph’s words made Allyne reel; she actually stumbled until he lifted a steadying hand to her elbow. Her father had never spoken of her mother – not once. Allyne had been starved for stories of her saintly dead mother, but her father had never before obliged her.

“Why,” Allyne blinked back tears, “did you never speak of her to me before?”

“I know I’ve not been a good father to you,” Randolph turned away from her tear-streaked face, his gaze lost somewhere over the Lake Michigan horizon. “I don’t talk about Alice to anyone. It’s been twenty-three years and still it hurts to think of her. Poor Allyne – you’d no chance with me. You look so much like your mother, it pains me. She died for you.”

“And you don’t think it was a fair exchange,” Allyne spoke bitterly.

“It’s . . . illogical,” her father stammered. “Your mother loved you – even if she only knew you for a few hours. I knew you were part of her, and my own flesh and blood. I promised Alice I would care for you, but I just couldn’t – ”

“Couldn’t love me,” Allyne let a sob escape.

“Couldn’t trust myself with the chance. I loved only one person ever and she left me. I promised your mother I would care for you and that’s what I’ve done; you’ve wanted for nothing.”

"Except love," Allyne made no effort to stop the tears now spilling over her lids. "But at least I understand now how hard it must have been for you. If I lost Cass..."

"Do you really love this meat packer's son?" Randolph asked with an air of getting the worst over as expediently as possible.

"I'm afraid I do," Allyne sighed.

"Then why are *you* afraid?"

"He's Catholic, his parents are Irish immigrants and his mother is quite vulgar, he lives in Chicago – he proclaims to enjoy being a meat packer."

"Those are the very reasons your grandmothers cited, but why are you afraid?"

"I could never live in the Midwest!"

"Why not? You hate New York. Why not start fresh as the leading lady of Chicago society?"

"I won't raise Catholic children."

"Your Grandmother Patsy once said the same thing about raising an Episcopalian, but she loves you even so."

"Do you approve, then?" Allyne asked hopefully.

"I ought to meet him first," her father declared, his tone firm.

"You'll meet him at the ball tonight."

"I hope I approve of him," her father declared, blinking back tears of his own as he finally turned to meet Allyne's eyes. ". . . if you love him. You deserve to be happy, Allyne."

Miss Verity Bennett and Mrs. Polly Easton exchanged glances after the awkward introductions to their dinner companions. Grand Hotel's *Salle à Manger* was at full capacity this Saturday evening and each available chair had been utilized. Unfortunately, Verity had been seen to voluntarily dine with Elizabeth and Bertha Collins often enough for the host to guide her and Polly to their table in the sprawling dining room. Obvious Transients filled the other two chairs – a mother and daughter, both with mousy complexions, thin, tawny hair and massive, brown eyes full of wonder for their opulent surroundings. Mrs. and Miss Visser also hailed from Peoria and were well acquainted with the Collins family, though Bertha Collins and Cecelia Visser looked decidedly less enthused by the connection than their elder relations. Polly's raised brows echoed Verity's mild condescension for the Vissers and amusement for Bertha's aversion to their presence.

How good it felt to exchange such companionable glances with her old friend again! Verity had missed meeting Polly's dancing, dark blue eyes – missed the shared scorn or hilarity she so often found there. No one knew her better or could read her thoughts like Polly.

"We're staying for a week," Miss Cecelia Visser answered Bertha's patronizing inquiry. "Or just over – we'll return to Peoria on Monday, the Fourth. I wonder if we'll take the same ship?"

"We won't," Bertha declared. "Many of the cottagers stay on the island through mid September."

"When will you be returning to Peoria?" Cecelia asked.

"I'm not certain," Bertha shrugged in imitation of sophisticated society lady. "I'll be spending some time this autumn with Miss Halloran—Miss Lillis Halloran—in

Chicago. I don't know there will be time for Peoria between leaving the island and my stay in Chicago."

Verity kept a sharp eye upon Elizabeth Collins to gauge the woman's reaction to her granddaughter's words. Elizabeth kept her eyes fixed upon her plate, pretending not to hear, refusing to acknowledge Bertha's boastful declarations. Verity couldn't wait to analyze the woman's reaction with Polly later this evening.

"Oh, it's beautiful! Thank you, Franklin!"

The exuberant cry from the first table by the windows drew Verity's gaze. She watched Priscilla Pruett's smile blossom as Mr. Pruett fastened the diamond bracelet over her wrist and – what was this? Priscilla willingly offered her cheek to be kissed. My, my – this was a development!

"Happy Birthday, darling," Franklin spoke in carrying voice as he reclaimed his chair and turned expectantly to the waiter popping their champagne cork.

Verity turned to see if Polly had noticed the Pruetts' very public exchange, but she was too politely engaged with the uninspiring occupants of their own table.

"Oh, yes – we knew them," Bertha's chest inflated with self-importance. "Such a tragedy."

"You mean we saw them," Mrs. Collins warily corrected her granddaughter. "We were not acquainted with the Harris family."

"I most certainly was," Bertha snapped. "In fact, Miss Bennett was with me when I was first introduced to Mrs. Harris. We played euchre all afternoon."

Verity's eyes narrowed at the memory. Oh, she remembered that euchre game – and how they would have won if not for Bertha's intentional renege so she could run after Miss Vandermeer and Mr. Drury. Deluged by sudden wave of guilt for harboring regret for not beating a murdered woman in a card game, Verity resolved to forgive Bertha.

"Yes, I remember the day," Verity nodded. "Rose Harris was such a sweet and beautiful woman, and so devoted to her children. I must say I had my suspicions that all was not as perfect as their public demeanor suggested, but no one could have imagined their horrific fate."

"They say Mr. Harris stabbed Mrs. Harris twenty-seven times," Miss Visser sounded a little too enthused for the gruesome subject.

"Twenty-seven *cuts*," Bertha corrected her. "Only three full stab wounds. I read most of the slashes were to her arms – she tried to fight him off, to save her children."

"Ladies, please," Polly admonished them. "Have some respect for the dead, not to mention that we are at a dinner table."

The young ladies murmured resentful apologies and fell to discussing some mutual Peoria acquaintance's recent engagement. Mrs. Collins and Mrs. Visser had long since fallen into rehashing the latest news from home, leaving Verity and Polly in peace to enjoy the rest of their meal.

"Well, look at that!" Even Polly could not help but notice the group strolling through the room's central columns past their table.

Allyne Vandermeer's tall, graceful figure always drew the eye; today she walked beside a rather gaunt, but distinguished man with salt and pepper hair and important-looking mahogany mustache. He was impeccably clad in tails and white tie and loped with the same easy grace he had bequeathed to his daughter. Still the tallest of the group—and decidedly the most handsome—Cass Kearney walked behind Allyne, escorting his sister, Anne. Patsy Webb and Lydia Vandermeer trailed after them, wearing equally sullen expressions.

"So Alice Webb's husband has finally taken an interest in his daughter," Verity nodded with grim satisfaction.

"About time, too," Polly agreed. "Patsy says it's shameful how he ignores Allyne in New York. She resents that Lydia hasn't properly taken Randolph to task for shirking his duty to the girl."

"Let's just hope he does the right thing now and gives their engagement his blessing."

"It is rather hasty, though," Polly remarked. "Just like her mother."

"She's truly in love with him."

"How do you know that?"

"She told me so," Verity replied. "And if you'd seen the size of that diamond on her finger, I'd say he loves her as much in return."

"Are you sure it's not a matter of spend a small fortune now to secure a larger one at the altar?"

"You've been spending too much time with Lydia and Patsy!" Verity bristled. "Did you know that Cass has refused to give up his position at the packing company? And insists they live in Chicago – at risk of losing her? Does that sound like a man after a fortune?"

"No," Polly acknowledged. "I'm sure you're right in the matter – and I certainly hope so."

Verity lifted the last bite of beef tenderloin to her lips and glanced up to find Bertha Collins staring with unpleasantly gaping mouth and flushed, round cheeks. Catching Verity's return gaze, Bertha quickly looked away. Yet from that point forward the girl seemed too distracted to maintain a normal conversation. Fortunately, they only had one more course to endure.

Half an hour later Verity and Polly claimed two of the plush chairs around the dance floor's perimeter in the Casino. Verity tapped her foot to the polka tune, less resentful of her lack of dancing partners with Polly at her side, listening to her critiques and observations of the younger ladies twirling across the floor.

"She's a fine dancer – I'll say that for Miss Lillis Halloran," Verity remarked. "That's her third dance with Mr. Drury – have you noticed? They look positively smitten. Allyne and Cass have better form, but Mr. Drury really carries Miss Halloran through the steps nicely. Would you look! Mr. and Mrs. Pruett seem to be retiring early this evening – and do you see his hand upon her back? That's the first she's let him touch her all summer. They must have resolved their quarrel. Ah, but Miss Collins is so heavy on her feet; I don't envy her dancing partner. And would you look at—"

"Verity," Polly gave her a light jab with her elbow.

"What?" Verity asked, cross to be so rudely interrupted and by how much pain she felt from that bony elbow.

"Miss Bennett?"

Her head snapped up to behold Mr. Randolph Vandermeer bowing in greeting.

"Excuse me – I don't believe we've been introduced?" Verity rose to her feet, but still the man towered over a foot above her head.

"Forgive my breach of protocol," Randolph Vandermeer—millionaire, business icon, friend of the President and half the Senate—spoke in timid, beseeching tone. "Allyne pointed you out to me, but I can't seem to pry her away from Mr. Kearney long enough for her to make the introduction. I'm Randolph Vandermeer."

"Yes," Verity nodded, waiting for him to further explain his presence at her side.

"My wife—my late wife, Alice Webb—spoke very highly of you."

"Alice Webb spoke highly of me?" Verity was truly taken aback.

"She said you were the best dancer in Bennettsville. She spent many summers there with her mother and she admired how you accepted every dance, even though you were—um—more mature than most of the other ladies, and that when you danced she forgot your age because you smiled as gaily as any of the young girls. You must have left quite an impression upon Alice, for she spoke of you to me more than once. 'I wish you could see Miss Bennett dance,' she told me several times. May I have your next dance, Miss Bennett?"

And finally Verity was swept around the dance floor, and Polly smiled for her good fortune, and this was the best night in at least three years.

Elliott Maier helped Iva step up into the phaeton, then squeezed beside her on the back bench next to Hugh and Agnes Pendleton; the irony of accepting a ride home from the Hallorans did not escape him. These particular Hallorans had elected to leave Grand Hotel's Saturday ball at the same time as Elliott's party. Well after midnight, muddled by wine over dinner, Elliott had dreaded the uphill trek back to the Annex and was only too relieved to accept the offer from Adelia's eldest brother, Joseph Halloran. His wife, Mary, daughter, Lillis, and niece, Alva filled the front bench beside him, their gay chatter drowning out the sound of crickets and jangling tack as Joseph guided the horses away from the hotel.

Elliott's gaze drifted above the treetops to the vast, starry sky as the carriage rumbled up West Bluff Road. This was the last Saturday ball from which he would ever drive home. On Friday Elliott would turn Mapleview's deed and keys over to Franklin Pruett.

Even as he grasped at the moments to enjoy, bitterness had pervaded Elliott's last Grand Hotel ball as a cottage owner. His old Annex friends that just two weeks ago had slapped his back on the baseball field averted their eyes from him tonight. His mere presence discomforted them – what did you say to the friend you grew up with now forced to sell his family cottage? No one should think of finances or economic conditions or anything so serious here on Mackinac Island and they resented Elliott for calling such matters to mind.

Of course Iva had been a saint all evening – pretending not to notice the wary glances, speaking cordially to

Agnes Pendleton and the other Annex ladies, accepting every dance request as though it were not offered in show of sympathy. Iva hadn't batted an eye when Elliott felt compelled to ask Adelia Halloran—Alston—for a dance.

Elliott had needed that last waltz. He would hand over Mapleview to Franklin Pruett on Friday and he would finally relinquish Adelia to Eli Alston. For him, Adelia and Mackinac were one; this was Elliott's only consolation in leaving the beloved island. He would finally bid Adelia Halloran goodbye.

Joseph Halloran reined in before Pendleton Pines and waited for Hugh and Agnes to alight. Elliott blinked back tears as he waved his old friend off. His parents were right about the demon liquor, for he was seldom afflicted with such emotion. Elliott blamed the wine over dinner. He turned to regard Iva as the carriage drew to a stop before Mapleview's front gate; she had consumed an equal measure of wine, yet seemed so cool and composed.

"Thank you for the ride home," Iva offered as Elliott helped her step from phaeton to carriage block.

She waved the Hallorans off and spun on her heel to march up the walk. The force with which Iva pushed open the front gate finally convinced Elliott that she also felt the wine's influence. He trudged up the walk after his wife, but she stopped suddenly at the foot of the porch steps, turning to meet his eyes in the moonlight.

"I hope tonight was the worst of it," rare flickers of passion deepened Iva's pragmatic voice.

Elliott welcomed her stern tone and flashing eyes – would his calm, composed wife finally express her anger and disdain? He had failed to provide for his family in the manner they deserved. He had earned her scorn, her rebuke.

"I'm sorry," Elliott hung his head. "I hoped you wouldn't feel it as keenly as I did – all their embarrassed, pitying glances. All summer they treated us as one of them, ignoring the looming fact that this was our last season at Mapleview."

"Do you think I care about Mapleview?" the vehemence in Iva's ordinarily sedate tone made Elliott stumble back from the porch step he climbed. "Do you think I care to keep a cottage haunted by another woman?"

"If you're . . . referring to Adelia—" Elliott stammered.

"No, you dunce! This was your mother's cottage! I feel her lurking over my shoulder in every room, rebuking my every adjustment to one of her possessions. But since you mention Adelia, I'll admit she's further reason for us to leave this island and never look back!"

"What do you mean?" Elliott frowned.

"The island's set you back; you've not been yourself all summer."

"I'm reminded of all I lost here – of my potential and subsequent failures. I never should have exposed you to our old neighbors in such a position. You must resent me for it, and I am truly sorry, Iva."

"Stop!" Iva bristled, shoving him off the step he had attempted to mount. "Stop being sorry! Don't you see that I care nothing for them? I don't care for their opinion! I don't care to keep this old cottage!"

"I've failed you," Elliott bowed his head, unable to meet her gleaming eyes.

"You are not a failure," Iva reached for him, burying

her fingers in his dark blond hair, pulling his face closer to hers. "Your father's bank failed – along with a hundred others across the country. Did you retreat to lick your wounds, bemoaning your cruel fate? Did you lose yourself in despair and end your life, abandoning your family in act of supreme cowardice? Or worse – snap like Harland Harris? Did you succumb to drink like so many, many men do? No – you studied the law and started your own practice. You speculated in real estate and stocks. You're nearly back on your feet – you would have been years ago had you not also been supporting your parents. And even in our most precarious years, you never let the children perceive your worries. We never went to bed hungry. We've always had a sound roof over our heads. And you call yourself a failure?"

Tears rolled slowly down Elliott's cheeks as he lifted his hands to cradle Iva's face – so pale and fierce and lovely in the moonlight.

"I don't deserve you," he sighed.

"Yes, Elliott – you do! Haven't you heard a word I've said? I'm proud to be your wife. I admire your high standard and your hard work to achieve it. And I admire you more for supporting us by your own brain and dedication, rather than something carelessly assumed from your father.

"I know you love Mapleview and are sad to let it go, but it's made you oversensitive. I saw no embarrassed or pitying glances bestowed upon you tonight. I saw poignancy – your old friends were well aware they might not see you here ever again, and they were sad. Because they hold you in high esteem."

"Now I think your perception a little clouded by—"

"It's not just my perception," Iva snapped. "What do you think Agnes and I spoke of all summer? Of course Hugh's so fond of you, but Agnes also gave me fair assessment of how each Annex neighbor felt. Aside from the Hallorans and their closest friends, you are admired here on Mackinac Island, Elliott. And you're admired in Kalamazoo. And I don't ever want to hear the word 'failure' from you again!"

To Elliott's further astonishment, Iva pulled his face to hers for an ardent, but tender kiss. He felt her tears when she pressed her cheek to his and wound her arms around his waist. Elliott's arms encompassed her narrow shoulders, crushing her slim, delicate frame to his chest, relieved to discover that she didn't break. She just squeezed him back with unexpected strength.

"And Elliott," Iva murmured as they slowly drew apart to meet each other's eyes. "I meant what I said about Adelia Halloran."

"Alston," he corrected his wife.

"I know you still think of her as Adelia Halloran – your first love, youth's ideal lady. And I never want to see her again."

"Neither do I," Elliott declared, drawing Iva back into his arms for another kiss.

And—for the first time in fifteen years—he meant it.

Eighteen

People who had come to know Bertha Collins that last summer of the nineteenth century on Mackinac Island noticed the change in her. They still admired her luxuriant, raven curls, but she seemed more pallid these days. Most young ladies of the island possessed a sun-kissed copper glow by summer's end, but Bertha's pale complexion looked waxen, dead. Her small, brown eyes had lost the vibrant gleam emanating from them all summer. Instead of marching through rooms, Bertha now drifted. People worried for her health and thought her grandmother should be more concerned.

Bertha cared nothing for their well-intentioned fretting. She knew her wan complexion and tired eyes were from lack of sleep. For the past five days—since her last encounter with Lillis—Bertha had stayed awake all night so she would get there before sunrise. She took long afternoon naps, but they failed to compensate for five nights of missing sleep.

Trudging past the old fort in the pearl-gray, pre-dawn light, Bertha's round cheeks flamed to recall her last exchange with Lillis Halloran. Bertha had bided her time all night – enduring Cecelia Visser's prattle and the indecently perceptive eyes of that old maid, Verity Bennett, over dinner. Lillis practically clung to Del in the Casino after dinner, but Bertha had managed to corner her in the powder room midway through last Saturday's ball.

"Allyne and Cass seem to be back on," Bertha had remarked, watching Lillis closely for her reaction to this development.

"Yes," Lillis had murmured absently, patting blonde wisps into place as she spared an appraising glance into the mirror.

"So Allyne agreed to live in Chicago once they're married?" Bertha had striven for casual tone, but Lillis' jade eyes had flashed back to meet hers in the mirror.

"She hasn't decided," Lillis had replied, striding from the powder room. "She'll stay with us this fall as she prepares for the wedding to see how she adjusts to Chicago. I know she'll love it."

"So Allyne will be your houseguest all autumn?" Bertha had cried, drawing a frowning, backward glance from Lillis.

"Yes, of course; she should be with Cass, and we can't let her stay at a hotel. I'm so happy for Allyne! She's truly found love, and Cass is such a capital gentleman. Of course I'm jealous she gets to be Anne's sister, but I'll be so glad to have her as an ally in Chicago. It will be very gay, having Allyne to attend all the balls and receptions with. She'll distract me from how much I'll miss Del. There he is – excuse me, Bertha. Have a wonderful evening."

Memory of Lillis flouncing across the Casino toward Del still infuriated Bertha. Lillis had wished her a "wonderful evening," but had no care for whether that wish manifested.

Laughing with Anne, Allyne and Cass, smiling in besotted intensity up at Del, Lillis had already forgotten her old friend, Bertha Collins. Lillis had avoided her ever since – ignoring her letters, never being "home" when Bertha called at Sunset Cottage.

Stumbling up the wooded path, the scope of her losses overwhelmed Bertha. She would not be invited to the Hallorans' Chicago mansion – Allyne Vandermeer would be their guest for autumn's duration. Bertha would therefore not meet the wealthy Chicago gentlemen she had intended to ensnare into marriage proposals. And Lillis wouldn't miss her, for she would have Allyne to distract her – to confide in and laugh with. No doubt Lillis would grow even closer to Anne Kearney over Allyne's wedding plans. Lillis would forget her old friend from Rosewood Seminary. They would part at summer's end with no defined plans to reunite. Lillis seemed content to walk away, untroubled by the thought that she might never again set eyes upon Bertha Collins. But Bertha wouldn't be forgotten so easily. She wouldn't let Lillis cast her aside. And she'd be damned if she let Allyne Vandermeer take her rightful place by Lillis' side in Chicago this fall.

So Bertha staggered up the trail leading to Arch Rock. Lillis came to the rock to watch the sunrise at least once a week—sometimes with her Aunt Adelia, sometimes with her cousin, Alva, or brother, Patrick—but most often alone. Lillis would be a captive audience, standing halfway up that limestone arch, unable to avoid Bertha's direct assault. Perhaps she would give Lillis a chance to explain, a chance to apologize…

Crouching behind a clump of trees just south of the limestone arch, Bertha waited with heightened senses for Lillis' approach. She recalled Lillis' every deceptive, evasive word – every false smile and chiding remark. Lillis hadn't appreciated the hair bracelet; she had withdrawn even further after that grand gesture, turning to Allyne and Del, retreating to the familiar comforts of Kitty, Alva and Anne Kearney. Lillis had so many friends, a sister and numerous cousins – would she even remember Bertha's devotion and sacrifice six months from now?

Lillis' shunning turned Bertha's expectations on their head. Visions of life as a Chicago society lady dissolved into nightmares of Peoria's best parlors. And how could she live without Lillis? She wouldn't know of Lillis' social triumphs, her little dramas and beaux, her exotic, international travels. Bertha couldn't imagine a week without a glimpse of Lillis' green eyes and devilish grin.

Why didn't Lillis feel the same? How could she flounce off into the sunset without a spare thought for Bertha? If she cared for Bertha at all, Lillis would recognize her friend's plight. But she didn't care, Bertha finally realized with mounting resentment. Lillis didn't care how much Bertha admired her, how Bertha had helped her with schoolwork at Rosewood, how she had introduced her to Allyne Vandermeer and fostered their friendship. Lillis Halloran was an ungrateful bitch. She didn't deserve to be happy – not when Bertha suffered the sting of humility and tasted the venom of rejection.

Fatigue fueled rage made Bertha's ears ring; she didn't hear her friend's approaching footsteps until Lillis was suddenly sweeping past, fearlessly approaching the narrow limestone arc. Arch Rock loomed one hundred forty-six feet above the shore. The view under the arch from the bluff top revealed pale turquoise water, a narrow ribbon of new shore road and the tawny rocks of the cliff's base – a view that made the faint-hearted wary of stepping too close to the cliff's edge. Only the bravest—or most reckless—dared to climb out toward the arch's base, let alone walk to its very center where Lillis now stood in the day's first rays of sun. She looked back over her shoulder, as though expecting to see someone. Bertha remained well concealed among the trees and Lillis finally surrendered her full attention to the golden sun rising over Lake Huron and the emerald islands dotting the Straits.

Ever so carefully, Bertha crept out of the trees. Her Indian moccasins purchased at a souvenir shop made little sound as she approached the arch's base. For a second, Bertha considered calling out to her friend – *Why have you forsaken me? Why do you prefer Allyne's company? Why won't you answer my letters?* But she knew why. Lillis didn't care for her.

Allyne didn't deserve Lillis' friendship. Allyne hadn't given her a special bracelet or helped with her schoolwork or listened to her practice her elocution lessons. And yet Allyne would spend months at the Halloran house in Chicago while Bertha could languish in Peoria or Timbuktu for all Lillis cared.

Lillis had accepted the bracelet, asked Bertha to spend that one weekend in Chicago, invited her to numerous entertainments this summer. She had led Bertha to believe she was a true friend; she had abused Bertha's faith, shaken her trust. Bertha had held such hopes for this summer! And Lillis had shredded them without a second thought – for now that she had Allyne Vandermeer, she no longer needed Bertha's friendship. She had tossed Bertha aside like an old brooch or a piece of garbage. And Bertha wouldn't have it.

If Lillis Halloran thought she could abandon Bertha to waltz off into the sunset with Del and Allyne and Anne, she was mistaken. Lillis wouldn't be waltzing anywhere – or even walking. What was left of her—after they scraped that lovely blonde head from the rocks so far below—would never dance again. Bertha felt her blood rise to color her cheeks as she broke into a sprint up that arch, her hands lifting to Lillis' narrow shoulders.

Del Drury hastened up the woods path, chastising himself for oversleeping. He and Lillis had vowed to meet at Arch Rock to watch the sunrise over Del's last Saturday on Mackinac Island. His funds almost exhausted, Del was forced to use their remainder on return passage to Indianapolis. His ship to Chicago left Monday morning. He would live with his mother and stepfather while he finished his novel. It could be published by Christmas and he would be in Chicago to claim Lillis by the turn of the century. 1900 – a new year, a new century, with a New Woman by his side!

He just hoped his lapse this morning didn't anger his New Woman too much. They hadn't left last night's hop until one o'clock; he never could have risen before the sunrise if he went to sleep. And Del had been inspired to write. He had just set his head down upon his arms to rest at five o'clock and suddenly it was six-forty-five and he only had fifteen minutes until he was supposed to meet Lillis.

Del's eyes lifted to the pale blue sky above the towering trees. He had already missed the sunrise, but would Lillis still be there? Would she wait for him?

Emerging from the white pine, oak and cedars, Del breathed a sigh of relief, immediately followed by a pang of apprehension. Lillis stood upon the arch's crown – foolish, fearless girl! So gorgeous, her blonde hair and white dress gilded by the morning sun, her shapely, slim figure poised like a swan about to take flight. The slightest wobble or slip would send her plunging one hundred and forty feet to the merciless rocks below. *She has good balance*, Del told himself, his throat very dry.

Suddenly another figure emerged from the trees, swiftly approaching Arch Rock's southern base. Why was Bertha Collins awake at this hour? And what a nuisance – always trailing after Lillis with those strange, sly eyes. But why on earth was Bertha here?

Del's mind—still fogged from his brief lapse into slumber—took a few seconds to process what he saw. Lillis lifted a hand to shade her eyes as she squinted into the sunrise; she seemed unaware that Bertha lurked just ten yards away. Bertha approached the arch's base, but paused – like a cat over a particularly fat mouse. Before Del could even form the thoughts—*Why did Bertha not announce herself? Why did she stand so close to Lillis without calling out?* —Bertha broke into a mad sprint up the arch, her hands rising as if—

Del stumbled in his haste and opened his mouth to cry out, but panic choked him. In a split second he realized Bertha's intention, doubted his realization, rediscovered it and cried out – but no sound escaped his throat.

"Lil—" he tried again, this time managing to inflict some volume into his cry. "Lillis!"

Bertha's hands were two feet from Lillis' unsuspecting shoulders when she heard his strangled cry. She spun around, flinging her arms up to evade Bertha's assault. Lillis—stunned by her current predicament—stumbled back, her foot slipping, but she managed to steady herself by clinging to Bertha's sturdy frame.

Del sprinted forward, his heart lodged in this throat, his limbs spurred on by pure adrenaline as he watched Bertha Collins try to push the woman he loved off the arch. Lillis put up a fight, yanking Bertha's hair back and trying to wrestle past her. Bertha's fingernails clawed Lillis' cheek, drawing a scream of pain and further burst of defiance from Lillis. Bertha's swinging arms and gnashing teeth had a ferocious, frenzied air, but Lillis was the golfer, the cyclist – the island princess with all the power. Lillis drove her crazed attacker back with a vehement push. Bertha reeled, took a couple uneven steps back in attempt to regain her balance, and slipped off the arch. Her shrieks filled the air for several seconds, but were swiftly silenced upon impact with the rocks far below.

Lillis stumbled into Del's arms. He pressed her against his chest as if he could meld her to his skin. He had been that close to losing her – he would never let her go. Never.

"Del," she sobbed. "I killed her!"

"She tried to kill you."

"But . . . they'll find the body and . . ." Lillis' hand rose to her left cheek, still stinging with the marks from Bertha's nails. "They'll see my face. And . . . they'll know I . . ."

"No one will know anything," Del's firm arm around her trembling shoulders guided Lillis away from the gruesome scene at the base of Arch Rock.

They walked in silence all the way back to Sunset Cottage on the island's opposite bluff. Del shared Lillis' dazed, stunned emotion. They hadn't properly processed this morning's events; they weren't quite ready to speak of them. Yet they clasped hands for the walk's duration. Del wondered if Lillis clung to him for support or numb reflex; for his part, he held her hand to assure himself that she walked beside him in flesh and blood—that hers was not the body mangled on the rocks beneath Arch Rock.

"We have to say something," Lillis finally broke their silence when they reached the Annex.

"Say something?" Del's fingers squeezed hers in show of silent support.

"To my parents. We'll have to tell them that I . . . that I . . ."

"You don't have to tell them yet. Let's think about this—"

"But her body's just . . . lying there—on those rocks. We have to let them know . . . "

"Let me tell them," Del offered, holding open the front gate for Lillis to pass through.

"Will you stay here with me?" Lillis paused halfway up the porch steps, turning back to meet his eyes.

"Of course."

"I don't want you to leave – I don't want to be alone."

"I'm not going anywhere," Del assured her, succumbing to his need to clutch her face and press his lips to hers.

Her arms wound around him with equal ferocity and longing. Del had never experienced such passion. Their kiss was not borne from physical desire, but a celebration of life – of the sheer joy of still standing here on this great earth, still able to breath in the other's scent and press their bodies together and kiss like this.

"What is the meaning of this?" Joseph Halloran's booming voice made Del and Lillis jump apart; Lillis' father flung open the screen door with such force that it slammed against the white shingled wall, sagging off its hinges. "Stand back, ye scoundrel! If you are not gone from my—"

"Papa . . . stop!" Lillis thrust herself between Del's retreating figure and her father's barreling advance. "I have to tell you something—"

Mr. Halloran paused for a second, but then his eyes and cheeks flamed afresh to behold the red marks across his daughter's fair cheek.

"He has dared raise a hand to you?" Mr. Halloran bellowed, pushing Lillis aside and running at Del.

"No! Stop! It wasn't him!" Lillis caught her father's arm just before he could swing it at Del. "It was Bertha Collins!"

"Joseph? Lillis?" Mrs. Halloran hastened out to the veranda. "Good gracious – what's this about?"

"Please," Del strove to instill calm with his even tone. "Something terrible has happened this morning. It's shaken both Lillis and I. Can we sit for a moment and tell you of it?"

Still eyeing Del suspiciously, Mr. Halloran reluctantly lowered his arm. Mrs. Halloran led them up the side veranda to a cluster of chairs at the west-facing end. Though only September 2, the morning air was crisp on this shaded side of the cottage. Del hastily removed his sweater and draped it over Lillis' trembling shoulders, but dared not touch her again under her parents' watchful, censorious eyes.

"What's happened?" Mrs. Halloran demanded of her daughter.

"Bertha—" Lillis managed. "She's . . . dead. I—"

"Such a terrible tragedy," Del spoke over Lillis. "Miss Collins took her own life this morning."

"What?" Lillis' parents turned to him with equally horrified and doubtful expressions.

"Lillis and I had planned to meet at Arch Rock this morning to watch the sunrise. She arrived before me and encountered Miss Collins in a state of desperation. Poor Bertha's been out of sorts for the last week. We've all noticed her unhealthy pallor and exaggerated melancholia, though none of us could have fathomed the depths of her despair. When Lillis realized her intention, she attempted to stop Bertha. I saw it all from up the path, but was unable to reach poor Bertha in time to save her from herself. Bertha threw Lillis off, clawing at her face like a savage—you see the mark. Then she turned and ran right up to the top of the arch before leaping to her death."

Mr. Halloran's shrewd, hazel eyes had been fixed upon Lillis throughout Del's explanation.

"Is that really what happened?" the older man demanded of his daughter.

"No!" Lillis sobbed, burying her face in her hands as she relayed the morning's events.

"I like his version better," Mr. Halloran declared not long after her conclusion, rising purposefully from his chair. "It's the best for all concerned. Better to be remembered as a tragic suicide than a deranged attempted murderess. And the constable will have fewer questions about a suicide. Let's go, then."

Del's gaze fell from Lillis to the hand Mr. Halloran had clamped over his shoulder.

"Come along, young man. I'll need your witness testimony for the constable."

"Must you go now—" Lillis' voice rose in distress as her father propelled Del up the veranda.

"They must," Del heard Mrs. Halloran comfort Lillis as Mr. Halloran guided him down the porch steps and across the lawn to the carriage house.

"You'll tell the constable what you told us earlier?" Mr. Halloran prompted ten minutes later as he drove his runabout up Lakeview Boulevard.

"Yes," Del assured him.

"If you hadn't been there this morning—" Mr. Halloran broke off with a shudder, unwilling to carry his thought further.

"I was," Del spoke firmly, in equal unwillingness to consider the alternative.

"I saw ye kiss her earlier," Del flushed with embarrassment for the older man's frank words. "Like she might disappear if ye didn't hold onto her tight. Just what are your intentions toward my daughter, Mr. Drury?"

NINETEEN

Mist shrouded Mackinac Island Monday morning as the *Manitou* pulled out of the small harbor. Elliott Maier stood at the railing, impervious to the dreary weather as he watched a freighter refill at the unsightly coal dock. Coal was a necessity, of course, but Elliott thought the industrial dock a blemish on his beloved island. There had been no offensive piles of coal when he visited Mackinac with his parents as a child.

"Will soldiers ever return to the fort?" Martin asked, drawing Elliott's gaze up to the long, graceful white walls guarding the harbor.

"Anything's possible," he replied, ruffling his son's mop of white-blonde hair.

"I hope those cannons don't fire on us now!" Martin's enthusiasm for the idea was evident in tone, if not words. "We'd go straight to the bottom! I could swim to shore; so could you, Father. But Mama and Daisy and Walter would go down with the ship."

"Your mother may look like a delicate flower, but she's a strong swimmer. She'd swim to shore with Walter on her back and I'd take Daisy," Elliott declared, delighting in his son's imaginative expression.

"I certainly would," Iva agreed, joining them at the railing with firm clasp of Walter and Daisy's small hands.

Elliott turned to meet her eyes, sharing a glance of solidarity and understanding with his wife. He saw strength and encouragement in her eyes today – and empathy; he saw pride and expectation, faith and love. He saw Iva's relief to leave Mackinac Island behind and sympathy for his last regrets.

"We'll be soaked through in this mist," Iva declared. "I'm taking the children inside – unless you wish us here with you?"

"No," Elliott's expression conveyed his gratitude; Iva was allowing him to bid the island farewell on his own, even as she reminded him of her constant support. "Go on – I'll join you shortly."

He watched his wife's slim figure as she huddled over their children, shepherding them out of the mist, and wondered how he had ever considered her fragile. Iva was a brick. Elliott never could have survived his recent travails without her.

The steamship picked up speed after rounding the breakwall and Elliott's gaze lifted inadvertently to the ostentatious white cottage predominating over West Bluff Road. He recognized Pine Bluff as Adelia's claim to the island—her flag planted upon its soil—and he ceded the land to her.

He would settle his remaining debts with the proceeds from Mapleview's sale; the flour mill he had recently invested in seemed to be in line for handsome returns, and he had a dozen clients awaiting his legal services back in Kalamazoo. Elliott looked forward to the new century that seemed so much closer at this end of summer. He looked forward to the home improvements that he could finally afford. He couldn't wait to visit a jeweler and buy some earrings or a bracelet for Iva. And Elliott would start a savings fund for their future amusements. He didn't want the expense and upkeep of another cottage; Elliott sought broader horizons. He had always wanted to tour Europe. But even if he could only take his family as far as Chicago, Elliott would be grateful for the venture. Wherever they went from here, they would experience it together with the same blank slate of optimism.

His gaze shifted to the long, austere, white-columned façade of Grand Hotel – growing smaller as the ship carried him through the Straits, away from the island. Elliott admired the vision, but the sight no longer made his heart swell. He would always retain fond memories of promenading along that porch – with Adelia, but also with Iva and their children. Yet he no longer felt any proprietorship for Grand Hotel. Adelia could have it; she had claimed it long ago. She had never required his capitulation – that had been solely Elliott's notion. Now he was finally ready to let it all go, to look forward and not back. Turning from the ship's railing, Elliott relinquished Mackinac Island to Adelia Alston.

"What about 'Pruett Pines'?" Gil suggested as Franklin guided the horses along Park Avenue, prancing past the grassy commons.

"Wouldn't that be a bit confusing, with Pendleton Pines directly behind us?" Franklin reminded his son.

"I *told* you, we are to call it 'Fairies' Forest Haven'," Emmeline insisted.

"We most certainly are *not*," Monty scoffed.

"Mother!" Emmeline cried with the indignation of an indulged eight-year-old. "You said you approved of the name!"

"I said it was a fair name," Priscilla corrected her daughter. "But it's also a mouthful. We need a less cumbersome name."

"Like 'Mapleview'," Monty muttered.

"What about 'Blue Cottage'!" Francis felt compelled to make a contribution to the family discussion.

"That's the stupidest name in the world," Emmeline mercilessly crushed her little brother's hopes.

"Emmeline!" Franklin and Priscilla spoke in unified chastisement, though Franklin let his wife complete the admonishment.

"I'm sorry," Emmeline apologized to Francis under parental coercion; her expression remained mutinous, her tone sullen.

"Here we are!" Franklin reined in before Mapleview's front gate.

Emmeline and Francis were the first to scramble from the carriage.

"Will you let them in?" Franklin handed Monty the key he had received from Elliott Maier earlier that morning.

"I suppose Mapleview would be the most diplomatic option," Priscilla sighed, watching their eldest sons jog up the front walk.

Franklin placed a restraining hand over his wife's forearm, drawing her close as he murmured in her ear, "Or we could call it 'Prissy's Pride'?"

Her eyes flashed in a flare of ire as she turned back to meet his, but she quickly countered with, "I thought we had decided upon 'Franklin's Folly'?"

"I think 'Franklin's Redemption' has a nicer ring to it," he declared, offering a hand to assist Priscilla from phaeton to carriage block.

"If you think last night enough to redeem yourself, you're mistaken," Priscilla spoke archly, throwing a coy smile over her shoulder. "You've so very much to atone for."

"I'll be sure to continue my efforts tonight," Franklin promised, catching her shoulders to press a light kiss to the soft skin at the back of her neck before continuing their stroll up the walk.

Franklin beamed, overwhelmed by his good fortune as he strolled through his newly acquired cottage. His children's enthusiasm for a new place, for its coming transformation and additional rooms, for the expectation of returning to this "Fairies' Haven" every summer filled Franklin with contentment and joy. He felt he did right by his family, buying this place – every summer they would be forced to spend in each other's company here on this little enchanted island. They would make many fond memories in this cottage.

There was assuredly some aspect of the sacred or magical about Mackinac Island. Franklin had ventured here to appease Prissy's wounded pride, to induce her to be civil to him. The most he had hoped to achieve this summer was to restore the tolerant harmony they had known prior to the unfortunate incident involving his mistresses in front of Holderson's Dry Goods Emporium. Never had Franklin dared to dream that his recent transgressions would lead to the restoration of his wife's affection. She had welcomed him back into her bed for the first time in five years! Not only had Priscilla genuinely forgiven him, she seemed to value him as she had not done in so many lonely, desolate months. She laughed at his jokes, returned his smiles, expressed interest in his words. His wife had returned to him this summer on Mackinac Island – for that, Franklin would forever love this beautiful northern land.

Mrs. Polly Easton stood at the railing beside Miss Verity Bennett as the ferry *Chippewa* carried them across the Straits to the train station in Mackinaw City. Polly smiled admiringly—and a bit wistfully—up at Grand Hotel's impressive line of white columns. She would miss this crisp fresh air, the various shades of blue – of sky, water and pale outline of the peninsula shores. She would miss the slower, more natural pace of island life. And she would miss her old friend, whose company she had not enjoyed until the last fortnight of their summer retreat.

"Poor Elizabeth," Verity remarked – not for the first time; she had seemed determined to compensate for her previous silence by talking Polly's ear off over the last two weeks. "She has ten grandsons, but Bertha was her only granddaughter."

"Perhaps her lack of experience raising girls led to her granddaughter's tragic demise," Polly suggested.

"I'm sure it did," Verity nodded. "I always thought Bertha Collins an odd girl. She didn't show her grandmother the proper respect, in my observation. Elizabeth seemed to indulge her whims and did nothing to rein in her headstrong impulses. And Bertha had an unhealthy preoccupation with that Lillis Halloran."

"Odd, yes, but she never seemed despairing to me," Polly remarked.

"I don't think it was a suicide," Verity declared.

"What?" Polly scoffed. "The constable declared it a suicide – there were witnesses to the event. And Elizabeth told us it was a suicide."

"Did you notice how those 'witnesses' were not at the ball that night?"

"No doubt because they were traumatized by the events they witnessed that morning!"

"No one has seen Miss Halloran since Saturday," Verity observed.

"Her friend just died; she is mourning Bertha's loss."

"Was Bertha really her friend, though? If she was Bertha's friend, why wouldn't Lillis receive or call upon Elizabeth Collins? Why would she refuse to comfort her friend's grieving grandmother? There's intrigue there – mark my words."

Polly smiled for her friend's perceptions, vivid imagination, and—of course—assurance that she was right in the matter. After enduring her silent fury all summer, followed by assault of Verity's every observation of their fellow Grand Hotel patrons from the time of their estrangement, Polly happily anticipated waving her old friend off on an eastbound train tomorrow. She loved Verity dearly and would miss her again after a week or two apart, but Polly welcomed the relative calm of her son's house. There she only had a daughter-in-law and three high-spirited grandchildren to contend with. Yet just now—as the morning's mist lifted and the western sky showed a promise of blue over the still, glassy Straits water—Polly enjoyed the banter and gossip with her best friend.

"What intrigue?" Polly challenged. "Do you think Lillis Halloran pushed Bertha Collins from that arch?"

"I think it more probable than suicide. And—God forgive my wicked thoughts—I once found the idea of pushing Miss Collins off a cliff very appealing," Verity acknowledged, remembering that euchre game. "But I think it more likely that Mr. Drury had a hand in it – he's such a strong, strapping lad. He could have easily overpowered Bertha Collins. He was the primary 'witness,' I understand. Of course Miss Halloran backs his story – she's in love with him."

"You can tell that from observing them at a couple balls?" Polly chided her friend, smiling to see Verity's cheeks flush in affront.

"Miss Vandermeer confirmed it, but yes – I've always been noted for my keen perceptions, as you are aware. Or perhaps you aren't? You being the opposite of keenly perceptive."

"I did observe Miss Vandermeer on the docks this morning, but she didn't seem to notice you," Polly quipped. "I thought you two were such confidants?"

"We said our goodbyes after services yesterday," Verity spoke in customarily lofty tone. "She was there this morning to bid her grandmothers farewell. Naturally I had no wish to impose upon their last moment together."

"Naturally – and your sympathetic discretion was also the only reason you avoided Patsy Webb and Lydia Vandermeer?"

"I took sufficient leave of them after church yesterday, as well," Verity declared through her reluctant grin. "Lydia Vandermeer is a cold, unfeeling woman. She condescends to Patsy and has no appreciation for the merits of any town that's not New York City."

"What?" Polly gasped. "Do you mean to say she was ignorant of Bennettsville's history and the illustrious family it's named for?"

"Go hang!" Verity snapped in rare use of slang.

Polly met her friend's narrowed, mahogany eyes and they both burst into a peal of giggles to rival any of their girlhood. Yes – she would miss Verity's company soon after waving her off on that eastbound train. Continuing their spirited discussion as they disembarked from the ferry and settled into their train compartment, Polly wondered where she and Verity would venture next summer.

TWENTY

Miss Allyne Vandermeer paced Sunset Cottage's veranda from rounded front corner to far western end. The afternoon sun bathed the golden oaks and scarlet maples in a meliorating light, gilding this autumnal beauty and making the sapphire Straits glisten as though dusted by shimmering gems. The view was exquisite – and yet Allyne had tired of it.

Nearly a month had passed since she had seen Cass. He had boarded a steamship for Chicago the same day Allyne sent her grandmothers back to New York. She was officially under the care of Mrs. Mary Halloran until her wedding day, and Mrs. Halloran shared Lillis' wish to stay on Mackinac Island until Del finished writing his book. Lillis' grandparents—Paddy and Nora Halloran—also remained at Lakeview Cottage, hosts of the budding novelist and future grandson-in-law, Delbert Drury. Eager to speed their departure timeframe, Allyne had copied out the first three chapters of Del's novel and sent them to her father with the request that he share them with his prominent publishing connections. The response arrived just yesterday – Harper & Brothers wished to publish Del's novel; they sent an advance against the remaining chapters.

Allyne drew her woolen, tartan shawl more snugly over her thin shoulders. The last day of September in northern Michigan had a decidedly fall feel, despite the abundant sunshine. The air might feel pleasant without that brisk, west wind. Yet Allyne would rather shiver in the cool air than be stuck in the parlor another day. The plush furnishings and crisp scent of a blazing fire in the hearth, lounging in windless, sun-warmed rooms, and admiring the whitecaps disturbing the sapphire Straits water through their clean windows – Allyne had initially appreciated these comforts of Sunset Cottage, but now they bored her. She had taken to pacing its veranda and marching restlessly through its rooms, not bothering to hide her impatience to leave her gracious hostess' home.

Allyne yearned for Cass. She missed how his coffee eyes regarded her with admiration and pride, his complete confidence in everything, the comforting, arousing sensation of being enveloped in his arms. Pleased as she was by Del's literary success and his betrothal to Lillis, Allyne resented that the creation of his novel delayed her reunion with Cass in Chicago. Couldn't Del just finish the damned book? He had devoted at least five hours a day for the last month to the blasted endeavor. He was in no hurry, for each day he extended the novel meant another glorious opportunity to frolic with Lillis over this lovely, fairy island.

Pausing at the west railing, her reflective gaze traveled over the water, past the peninsula points to the Lake Michigan horizon. Anxious as she was to join Cass in

Chicago, Allyne acknowledged that she would rather be here than any alternative locale. She had no desire to ever visit New York or Newport again – well, perhaps after she married to show off her tall, devastatingly handsome husband . . . How envious the ladies would be! And let them dare disparage Cass to her. She was rather fatigued with foreign languages and impoverished aristocrats, though of course she looked forward to showing Cass her favorite European sights. Allyne thought she might like to visit California one day, but for now Mackinac Island was the only place for her – in her mind, the closest civilized location to Chicago.

Allyne and Cass had reached a grand compromise before his return to the demands of Kearney Packing. Cass consented to Allyne raising their children in the Episcopalian church; she said he could teach them the lessons and traditions of his Catholic faith. She acknowledged the fundamental significance of his career and agreed to live in Chicago; he promised they would travel for two months of each year. They had agreed upon the first Saturday of December for their wedding date. Allyne had realized over the last few weeks that she would agree to much more to be with Cass again.

Grandmother Vandermeer and Grandmother Webb were ashamed of her "impetuous decision" and "diminishing standards," so Allyne sent them away. For the first time in her young life, Allyne was left to her own devices, free from oppressive prejudices and stiff rebukes. She had her father's blessing in this matter, for Randolph Vandermeer approved of Cassius Kearney. Her father had not withheld any display of gratitude for the man he thought worthy to relieve him of his daughter's care. Randolph had promised Allyne the most lavish trousseau of any society miss, a new yacht to carry them on their first trip abroad, and to walk her down the aisle the first Saturday in December.

Allyne felt on the cusp of realized dreams, yet she had been kept from her beloved by Del's inability—or unwillingness—to finish that damned novel. At least Lillis' mother and grandparents had also lost patience. Their family had retreated south, every neighboring cottage had been shut up for the long winter, Grand Hotel had been closed for weeks, and the Hallorans would be sailing their yacht—*Northern Spirit*—south the first Monday of October. At least it wasn't long now; in approximately forty-eight hours, Allyne would be reunited with Cass. Stepping through the parlor's west doors, Allyne resolved to be gracious these last hours on Mackinac Island.

Del Drury swelled with a sense of accomplishment as he set his pen down over the last page of his first novel. Perhaps upon rereading and editing he would discover that it was not his masterpiece, but Del knew it was good. And—thanks to Allyne Vandermeer's impatience and good heart—he had the rare luxury of knowing the words he had just written would be published.

Lifting his eyes from the paper, Del took in the view. He had been given the west-facing third floor tower room of Lakeview Cottage with full leave to rearrange its furniture. Del had pulled the desk before the central windows. They were closed today against the cool wind, but still offered inspiring views of lake and sky. Just now the majestic beauty of the Straits awed Del.

He could never have imagined when he came to this island as a despairing life insurance agent that in less than three months he would be a guest of Lakeview Cottage, engaged to Chicago's most beautiful debutant, and on the brink of having his debut novel published. Del came to Mackinac Island to resign himself to an unwelcome fate and found a new destiny instead. And what a tumultuous journey he had undertaken to land here – in this spacious tower room of one of the island's grandest cottages! He had experienced passion and fallen in love this summer; finally knowing these emotions gave a deeper, more genuine tenor to Del's writing. His writing had always been technically sound, his prose witty, even humorous at times, but in this novel, Del's characters finally had depth. They would evoke an emotional response in the reader – at least Del hoped they would.

He was further awed to have summoned the concentration to write at all this past month living in Lillis' grandparents' cottage. When Nora Halloran wasn't trying to feed him or fawn over him, Paddy Halloran used the excuse of sharing a drink to impress upon him the family's high expectations. Del learned the family's history from Paddy, was treated to a glowing list of Lillis' attributes, and warned of the dire consequences he would face if he did not care for her as she deserved to be cared for. Then there was Lillis herself – beautiful, vivacious, fun, captivating Lillis. Yet Lillis inspired him as much as she distracted him. Del had no choice but to focus on his novel; he must succeed with it to be worthy of her.

Pushing back from the desk, Del rose to stretch his aching, ill-used muscles. Glancing through the south window he saw Allyne Vandermeer pacing the neighboring veranda, her skirts and shawl flapping in the brisk breeze. She looked miserable, but finally came to her senses and stepped inside.

Slipping into his navy blazer and smashing a straw boater over his chestnut hair, Del jogged downstairs and across the lawn to Sunset Cottage. He found Lillis and Allyne reclined in desultory poses atop the room's plushest chairs. Allyne lifted her brows in greeting, but Lillis sprang to her feet and glided across the rug toward him. Her bright, expectant expression revealed knowledge of his good tidings.

"Did you finish your novel?" she asked before he could blurt out the news.

"I did," he grinned.

"How wonderful!" Lillis drew his face close for a congratulatory kiss. "We must celebrate! I'll ask Grandpa to serve champagne for our dinner tonight."

"Your smile is all the celebration I need," Del declared.

"But we mustn't refuse an offer of champagne," Allyne spoke up to remind them of her presence.

"To Del's first novel!" Lillis offered the first champagne toast at her grandparents' dinner table two hours later.

The sunset sky—a mesh of vibrant pink and searing orange—cast the wood paneled room in rosy glow. A fire crackled in the hearth, its flickering light dancing over his dinner companions' jolly faces. Paddy and Nora Halloran took the head and foot of the long, mahogany table. Del and Lillis sat with their backs to the fireplace, facing Allyne and Mrs. Joseph Halloran. They all raised their glasses to echo Lillis' toast.

"To Lillis!" Del lifted his glass again after drinking to his novel. "My inspiration!"

"To both of ye!" Paddy Halloran bellowed. "To your engagement!"

"And to Allyne!" Del made another toast once their champagne coupes were refilled. "There would be no first novel without her. Grateful as I am for that, I am most in her debt for introducing me to Lillis. I wouldn't be standing here today if not for Allyne."

"To Allyne!" they chorused, making the aloof beauty flush with warmth and pride and affection as she graciously accepted the accolades.

"To the magic of Mackinac Island!" Allyne raised her coupe for one last toast. "To the spirits that drew us here to captivate and change us forever. May they never leave Mackinac!"

"They won't," Nora Halloran assured her younger guests. "This is the fairy island."

"To Mackinac!"

About the Author

Shana Osler is a native of Rochester, Michigan and currently resides in Shelby Township. She earned her communications degree from Boston University and has an established career in the marketing industry. Writing has always been her passion and favorite pastime. Northern Michigan—and Mackinac Island in particular—is one of her favorite travel destinations. This is her first formally published work.